Behavior Modification
for Horses

Series Title

Got Carrots?

Behavior Modification for Horses

A Positive Method for Training Horses

*Patti Dammier with illustrations
by Wendy Peabody*

Writers Club Press
San Jose New York Lincoln Shanghai

Behavior Modification for Horses
A Positive Method for Training Horses

Writers Club Press
an imprint of iUniverse.com, Inc.

For information address:
iUniverse.com, Inc.
5220 S 16th, Ste. 200
Lincoln, NE 68512
www.iuniverse.com

ISBN: 0-595-16305-X

Printed in the United States of America

To my husband, Ernie, a very special source of encouragement, my mother, Marion, who taught me to love and respect animals, and Xerxio, a gifted and wonderful horse, one of many who inspired me in my pursuit.

Epigraph

Horses should be trained in such a way that they not only love their riders but look forward to the time they are with them.

—Xenophon 400 B.C.

Contents

List of Illustrations

List of Tables

Preface

My pursuit of creating positive educational environments that support learning has lead to a lifelong study both experiential and academic. People or animals engage in activities that are pleasant and are encouraged to repeat those activities because they're pleasant. There is nothing mysterious about how learning takes place and the methods that will reinforce those preferred behaviors. Just because horse training claims to be natural doesn't mean it's an effective tool for creating a learning environment for horses. Horses accept our intervention because they learn through a series of positive experiences that no harm comes to them and we are consistent in our positive behavior. Research demonstrates that horses respond favorably to humans because we create a positive relationship.

It's time to move away from the faddish and quick fix methods and invest a little time to learn the **basic principles of**

behavior modification-that teaches anyone to create a **positive** learning environment and a method of obtaining desirable behavior from horses.

Acknowledgements

Writing a book takes more than a single person's effort. I would like to acknowledge the support and help of the following people:

Drs. Fred. A. Crowell and Ernest H. Dammier for academic support. Without their untiring efforts to assist in editing and content suggestions, this project wouldn't have been possible.

Wendy Peabody for her imaginative illustrations. Wendy is a freelance illustrator and fine artist who uses a wide variety of mediums, ranging from award winning sidewalk art done in colored pastels to computer graphics. Her favored medium is pen and ink, because of her working often in the black and white realm of comics. She is presently working on a project involving the publication of her own fantasy comic book series, the Dragonytes.

Growing up in Spain and traveling throughout Europe, she was strongly influenced by the art of the Early Byzantine to the Renaissance periods, and the observations of the Andalucian and Arabian horse. She majored in Media Arts and Illustration at the School of Visual Arts in Manhattan, New York, which further improved that which had been previously self taught. Her work can be seen online at www.dragonytes.com

Introduction: Behavioral Science For All Horse Disciplines

Take every horse training book you've read and make them really work.

This book is written for the rider or trainer who wants to understand the why behind the training or the tricks. It also provides the explanation behind any method of horse training and teaches trainers control of their horse training situation. It will give examples from most horse disciplines and the understandable basics to explain why they work. By being able to analyze horse training situations, riders/trainers have the power to create their own methods and procedures, and can analyze why a catchy trick doesn't continue to work.

Most books are dependent on catchy, tricky themes to capture audiences looking for a quick fix. There are also many classical books going back as far a Xenophon of ancient Greece, that provide excellent descriptions of classical training as well as recent publications with mysterious titles addressing horse whispering. All of these books may provide numerous explanations, but not the step-by-step analysis of the procedures that allow any animal to be trained in a sequential manner. There are some outstanding exceptions that are the yardstick of basic training and some are listed in the reference list. As in all excellent educational environments there are no mysteries, only understandable techniques that are practiced with patience. This foundation of explainable understandable work was developed by behavioral scientists. Even though most of this work was developed in labs using small animals the principles may be used to explain and understand all disciplines training horses.

Behavioral Science Works With All Disciplines

Whether it's Western, English, Dressage, or circus tricks, most of the world-renowned horse training is done with complete knowledge or an intuitive knowledge of behavioral methods. Horse training has been written about in many books but with few exceptions the details of behavioral training explanations seems to be left out. Most readers will be familiar with the behavioral training of dogs, dolphins, and circus animals, but are unfamiliar with how this can be used with a horse. Indeed horses possess a different personality and horse specific behavior than other animals that are predominately handled on the ground. There is a very easy application that can be used.

The shocking misconceptions that lead most trainers to rely on force rather than rewards are still a sad commentary on how little an impact behavioral science has had on the 21st century horse world. Some of this is due to historical reasons and an "old wives tales" approach to horse training. There are many common examples of the lack of understanding seen in the mistaken ideas that riders and trainers have for what constitutes a reward and punishment. The increase of unscientific hype and "quick fix" mentality among equestrian groups doesn't further the cause for better horse training methods. How often does one see that big loud pat on the shoulder of the horse accompanied with the loud "good boy/girl" comment and the rider thinks that the horse has been rewarded? This is absolute nonsense and makes just as little sense to the horse unless done with other actions to be explained in this book. Horses do provide some unique aspects, yet there is no mystery to understanding the sequence of shaping desirable behavior from your horse or diminishing those undesirable behaviors. Part I explains the basic principles to change behavior using **behavior modification** as applied to horses. Part II adds additional material based on the foundation outlined in Part I. Lastly, Part III gives several horse training studies that sequentially and specifically outline common training situations.

Most riders are taught by repetition of patterns they memorize. These patterns can work in your favor as in the example of the hours of repetition necessary to learn rider aids and the physical ability to sit the horse's gaits. Nevertheless, these aids often don't get results. Think twice about going back to clinics or training sessions where the clinician keeps you running around and neither the horse nor the rider is reinforced, or rewarded for appropriate behavior, and that doesn't mean the "slap-good horse". In other words a lesson goal is set, the horse or the rider understands and obtains it, and the instructor finds means to reinforce or insure that that behavior will be repeated. There are ways to look at the rider or training aids to ensure they get results. One of the ways is to understand appropriate goal setting and the other is to understand the tools of behavioral science.

As stated, **behavioral science** systematically studies the behavior of organisms. Horses like all animals, including humans, tend to repeat pleasurable happenings and avoid those that are unpleasant. Remember biology class experiments and the dish of paramecium? Swim to the food-swim away from the acid. Any action from the rider/trainer with a horse will either get the horse to repeat the action or not repeat it (or the horse to get his rider to repeat or not repeat the action). Sounds simple? It is. The first part of this book will review the specifics of behavioral training as it works for riders and horses and how you can stop having your horse train you.

1. Horse Training

After explaining basic behavioral techniques, the applications of those techniques on the ground and in the saddle are examples explained. Other aspects discussed are the relationship of the horse and trainer and how behavioral science effects this relationship. Additional resources included are the behavioral explanations about using training aids and the common horse training literature explained using step-by-step procedures using the outlined techniques, charts, and key points.

Key Points

- This book is written for the rider/trainer who wants to understand the why does it work or cause–effect relationship behind the training and the tricks.
- Provides the explanation behind **any** method of horse training and teaches readers to be in control of their horse training situation.
- By being able to analyze every horse training situation, the rider/trainer has the power to create unique methods or procedures and analyze why a catchy trick doesn't continue to work.
- The shocking misconception that leads most trainers to rely on force rather than rewards is still a sad commentary in the 21st century horse world; it doesn't have to be that way.
- Horses do provide some unique aspects, but there is no mystery to understand the sequence of shaping desirable behavior from your horse or diminishing those undesirable behaviors.
- Any action from the rider/trainer with a horse will either get the horse to repeat the action or not repeat it (or the horse to get his rider to repeat or not repeat the action).
- **Behavioral science** systematically studies the behavior of organisms and horses like all animals, including us, tend to repeat pleasurable happenings and avoid those that are unpleasant.

Part One:

Basic Tools Using Behavior Modification with Horses

1. Behavior Science: What Does It Offer for Training Horses?

> As the Artist must know what he wishes
> to convey by his completed work and the
> workman must understand how best to
> use his tools so must the rider have an
> exact knowledge of his aim and the way
> and means to obtain it.
>
> —Alois Podhasky

Behind every excellent trainer or rider there is knowledge either gained by the repetition of what works or the more formalized training in behavioral science. What does behavioral science have to offer someone training a horse? As a beginning explanation, behavioral science offers the trainer the methods of understanding how to get the horse to repeat desirable actions. (For greater detail, the definitions of the bold words will also be provided to give greater understanding of each concept.) Everyone working with horses has goals or training plans they want to achieve. Behavioral science offers the tools to achieve those goals and plans.

The advantage of taking the time to understand behavioral methods is to take control of all training rather than rely on an explanation of only one type of training. All training can be explained and analyzed through behavioral science. The isolated techniques of this approach or that approach only apply to the exact examples or sets of examples and don't give the absolute control to the trainer to understand what is occurring in the pattern of behavior. The other advantage is that once a trainer understands this material, all other methods can be used and changed to fit the exact set of circumstances. Once a trainer masters some simple concepts, everything that is done will be seen as systematic sequential training, including riding, and not just the isolated methods learned from a "how to" book.

Training Method Failure Explained

How many times do trainers get excited about the new techniques only to find after they returned home from the clinic it doesn't work for them or their horse? It isn't always the fault of the clinician or the method for the failure. Many times failure lies in the difficulty in reproducing the exact training setting or environment. When a training method doesn't work, it's generally assumed that another method will be better. Trainers/riders are often seen running from one new idea to the next hoping to find what they need.

We have the answer if the tools of behavioral science are applied. Behavioral science is the key to understanding any type of training done with horses. In addition, behavioral science considers the learning environment, focusing on the skills to be taught or learned. Also considered is the education of the trainer and the training that produces step-by-step tasks that will yield specific goals. If the training method that has been learned doesn't work, it may just be "smoke and mirrors" and not have any valid educational value. Armed with behavioral science you will know the difference.

Preliminary Ideas About Learning

There's much written about how people and animals learn. Unfortunately some of the literature is either not specific and in general terms, or is too technical to reproduce in most training surroundings. However, there's much from behavioral science to use in the successful training of horses that leads to enjoyment and a happier experience for both partners.

Much of the theory developed in labs has a practical application and can be successfully used with a little self-taught knowledge and practice. To understand it is necessary to be aware of the principles of how organisms learn and are motivated to learn, and seek a cause effect relationship in observable behavior. The quantity of long scientific names to describe this process often discourages the layperson from using behavioral training. The trainer, however can be equally as accurate as the lab scientist, by merely understanding some basic principles that encourage or discourage all organisms to repeat or not repeat certain behaviors. Understanding some of these basic principles will allow us to become more successful and kinder when dealing with our friend the horse. This book outlines the basic concepts and tools used by scientists and how they may be used by the trainer or rider toward this end.

Key Points

- Behind every excellent trainer or rider there is knowledge either gained by the repetition of what works, or the formalized training of behavioral science.
- When riders ride, they're training the horse; the horse will remember that exercise positively or negatively. Every ride is a training session.

- Behavioral science is the key to understanding and explains **any** type of training done with horses so that the actions can be duplicated.

- There's much from the behavioral science to use in the successful training of horses that leads to enjoyment and a happier experience for both partners.

- Understanding some basic principles will allow us to become more successful and kinder when dealing with our friend the horse.

- **Behavioral Science:** The systematic study and observation of the behavior of organisms and the discovery of the order of how certain events of behavior follow relations to other events (B. F. Skinner, 1965, p.6)

2. Review of Behavior Modification As Applied to Horses

Learning is a relatively durable change in behavior or knowledge

—*Weiten*

Behavioral modification is a neutral powerful tool. It doesn't take on a good or bad connotation until used by the trainer, and it exists whether we make a conscious effort to use it or not. The arrangement between the surroundings, organisms like horses and people, and the cue or stimulus that encourages or discourages behavior is always present. Behavior always exists, so we can choose to work with it in a positive manner if we train ourselves and are knowledgeable. A trainer can also make the decision to wait for the behavior to naturally occur. Just because behavior occurs naturally doesn't mean it's better.

2. Natural Method of Training

Natural horse training methods...wait a long time.
Just because something occurs naturally doesn't mean it's better or what we want.

Observable behavior can be systematically to our advantage by understanding the sequence. Our animals ultimately have no choice in the matter and so the better trained, the better their existence. There are many trainers using these unexplained techniques to better the lives of horses. Horse training books though aren't reaching their full effect because they haven't been explained in behavioral techniques that allow for a step-by-step breakdown of how the behavior was reinforced or encouraged. Animals perform the desired behavior because they have been correctly reinforced for that performance (or not correctly reinforced). An example of this is an ex-bronco whose only idea was that humans were his nemesis and the best thing he could do was to get rid of them. Unless he changed his behavior he was doomed to be put to sleep. Enter behavioral training and a happy ending (see Part III). The goal was to have a well-behaved riding horse. Behavioral science can train or retrain a living organism to perform behavior by the systematic use of reinforcers that change behavior.

A horse can't run around as a bronco and be calm and well behaved at the same time. These are incompatible behaviors. Animals can't perform opposite behaviors at the same time, so when desirable behavior is consistently trained, undesirable performance is reduced and eliminated. If we are able to analyze our goals in terms of the specific observable tasks or behavior we want from our horses; this begins the first part of the training tools. The following section is a brief description of the training tools used in behavioral training and some commonly found examples of their use with horses.

Key Points

- Behavioral modification is a neutral powerful tool. It doesn't take on a good or bad connotation, until used by the trainer. It exists whether we make a conscious effort to use it or not.
- Behavior always exists, so we can choose to work with it in a positive manner if we train ourselves and are knowledgeable.
- Behavior of animals isn't mystical or haphazard, but is systematically changed by everything in the surroundings.

Establishing the Learning Environment: Setting Goals and Objectives

The first step is to have a clear defined understanding of what we want to achieve. How is successful performance described or defined? This demands an exact statement of the observable performed tasks needed to be taught. Riders and trainers often set large broad goals, but fail to break these goals down into the smallest possible objective or successful act the horse can perform. Not only is it essential to have a clear picture of the broad **goal** of your training, but also the small steps that lead to that goal. So the next time you are involved in riding/training lesson, ask what the goal of the lesson is and the successive steps or observable behavior that will be asked to demonstrate that goal. This is also the way that the trainer knows if the goals or objectives have been reached. The method that allows the trainer to retreat to an easier objective or observable act to retrain is important. Any teacher worth a salary walks into the classroom with a lesson plan. If you are training your horse, walk into that training session with a lesson plan or at least a clear idea of what exactly the horse is to perform. Often trainers leap to the larger goal without going through the small successive steps or **objectives** that allow that goal to be reached. They know they want to jump over a huge fence or perform multiple flying changes, but fail to outline the small successive steps of learning that lead to the large overall picture.

Key Points

- A series of small steps or objectives allow the trainer to obtain the broader or larger goal.
- The first important step is to identify the smallest observable behavior that can be performed. If it cannot be performed successfully then a smaller step must be redefined.

3. Goals and Objectives

Goals
*Broad description of the whole training lesson
in comparison to objectives.*

Objectives
The smaller well defined behaviors
that lead to the big goal or overall training plan

Contingencies-What Are They?

Many trainers know about using what is commonly called the "carrot" and stick" method of training, but what isn't understood is that there are vital specifics that make this work or, even more to the point, don't make it work. The main ideas behind animal behavior and human behavior as well, are explained by the exact use of contingencies. A contingency as used in the experimental work of behavior scientists, states that there is a relationship to how an animal will learn a specific behavior. The desired behavior will be the direct results of how the major parts of **operant conditioning** are applied. The major parts of a contingency are: the stimulus, the response or observed behavior, and the consequences (reinforcer/punisher). The method used by operant conditioning makes use of these contingencies to obtain desired behavior. The significant part is an understanding of how contingencies operate so that a trainer may encourage or discourage behavior change. There are some extremely important aspects that make these methods work and create the desired behavior. In the case of the "stick" method, which is unfortunately favored by many trainers, this may later produce poor results that detract from the desired training. These results often aren't apparent immediately and in the case of horses, very difficult to change and sometimes never change. The important lost confidence is often never regained. **Contingencies** are the systematic procedures of working with the desired responses and the happenings or consequences that follow the behavior. The type of **contingency** (rewarding or punishing) that is used and how it is used will be the critical factor as to whether our partner, the horse, will remain our friend or foe.

Key Points

- Contingencies are the operating procedures that effect a behavior that will encourage/discourage occurrence in the future.
- The type of contingency that is used and how it is used will be the critical factor as to whether or not the horse will remain our friend or foe.

A Brief Overview of Behavioral Science

Pavlov started most of the work in the area of behavior science. He began his work with dogs studying the effects of digestion. His work is almost always given as an example of training by citing the example of ringing a bell to cause an organism to perform a behavior. Although this provided the start, it is an example of **classical conditioning** of **natural reflexes.** It was actually Watson, Thorndike, and B. F. Skinner who provided much of the work developed in experiments used in animal training, called **operant conditioning.** This is the method that allows the training to change or **shape** behaviors that aren't always found naturally in the animal as in natural **reflexes,** like the salivation of Pavlov's dogs. Unfortunately horses unlike mice and pigeons don't fit into labs very well, and this may be the partial reason for the lack of literature using behavioral conditioning or management with horses. The other aspect is that much of the training and books written about training horses is accomplished while riding the horse. While there is more written about dogs and other animals, most of what is written about horses is behaviorally sketchy or written in journals not accessed by the public or easily implemented. Generally the lab work testing the intelligence of horses traditionally tests the ability to discriminate among symbols or run mazes to obtain a food reward. These types of experiments don't appear to have much use for the average horse trainer. Additionally, the experiments that are synopsized for the layperson aren't always understandable in terms or explained in ways that may be useful in settings outside controlled research environments (A list of materials is found at the appendix for more in-depth reading). The focus of this book is to explain how these powerful techniques may be used teach horses to perform.

Key Points

- The history of the lab work done in behavior science can provide answers to how horses may be more effectively and humanely trained.
- Operant conditioning allows the training to change or shape behaviors that aren't always found naturally in the animal like in natural reflexes; behavior they normally display in their own setting.

Behavior and the Environment

Organisms are always interacting with the environment around them. Whether this interaction is noted or ignored, it occurs. Most of this interaction happens in a haphazard fashion, and is occasionally noted or given an internal, emotional, or mysterious explanation, when in fact it may be observed, explained, planned, and encouraged. Behavioral science takes notice of this cause-effect interaction and basically says behavior doesn't have to be left to chance. A beneficial tool is provided, as trainers take notice of the interaction of the environment and their horse's behavior and begin systematically to encourage desirable behavior. Behavior may be changed in a systematic procedure and provides a tool for encouraging the best horse behavior possible. Behavioral science presents a tool that is totally neutral until the trainer decides upon the behavior desired and how it will be encouraged. The positive outcome of not leaving behavior to chance is to ensure that our partner and friend is better behaved, and becomes more likable and fun to be around.

Key Points

- Organisms are always interacting with the environment around them. Whether this interaction is noted or ignored, it occurs.
- The realization that behavior may be changed by the use of a systematic procedure provides the trainer with tools for encouraging the best horse behavior possible.

Basics of Changing Your Horse's Behavior

Whether an active choice is made or not the **environment** changes continually and behavior responds to those changes; it starts to rain and we grab an umbrella before we go outside. This is an example of random happenings in the environment and an unplanned response. There is a better way rather than a random happening; the response can be made more predictable. Skinner explains in these short sentences: that behavior occurs because of some reason; behavior that occurs and is followed by a consequence is likely to occur again; if there was a stimulus present at the time, there is a higher probability that the behavior will occur in similar situations when that same stimulus is presented in those similar situations. If we want horses to complete desired behavior, the trainer seeks to ensure that all of the following elements stimulus, behavior, and consequences are present: All areas are important.

1. Table: Stimulus, Behavior, and Consequence

Stimulus	Behavior	Consequence
The trainer decides on a signal or some kind of cue that is obvious to the horse-could be visual-showing the halter, sound-whistle	The horse performs an observable action that the trainer wants	An effect or action that happens to the horse right after the behavior the horse performs

Key Points

• If you want a behavior to reoccur, you create the same situation, using the same cues or actions that are called a stimulus and consequence.

Consequences or Outcomes Using Reinforcers

Reinforcers influence behavior or the actions we want the horse to perform. These actions or consequences occurring after the behavior will strengthen the horse's response or increase the rate of responding. Reinforcers may be positive or negative, but both increase behavior that precedes the reinforcer. In the next chapters each reinforcer and the effect on horse training will be described. Most trainers think they understand the "carrot and stick method" but mostly rely on the stick rather than the carrot. There are reasons to explain this behavior as discussed later in this book. Positive reinforcers have the advantage of producing confidence and stability in the partnership. Since the focus of the training relationship is to foster confidence in the trainer, the focus of this book is positive reinforcers. An example of a positive reinforcer is a carrot. Animals tend to repeat those acts that bring pleasure. The horse comes; a carrot is **immediately** given so a **connection with the behavior** is made. Rewards or positive reinforcers for horses may start with food and progressively become more complicated schedules as discussed later in this book. The important idea is to understand that reinforcers are pleasurable events that encourage behavior to repeat. To think of this in simple terms:

2. Table: Behavior and Reinforcers

Desired **Behavior** The trainer decides on a simple behavior for the horse to perform	Positive Reinforcers - Something pleasant given or done to the horse **immediately** after the behavior-increase behavior

Key Points

- Behavioral scientists state precisely the reasons why the "carrot" and "stick" method work and dispel the myths and misconceptions attached with the methods.
- The focus of the training relationship is to foster confidence in the trainer, and the use of positive reinforcers.
- Reinforcers strengthen the response or increase the rate of responding.

Primary and Secondary Reinforcers

There are popularized methods of horse training that are based on operant conditioning, but not explained in a manner that allows replication. Many of these methods have been effectively used with other animals. As stated previously horses bring other aspects to the training environment that make it different than animals that are primarily worked with on the ground. Animals that are worked on the ground primarily move to objects when directed by cues. Some of the same work done with other animals on the ground also works for tasks when handling the horse on the ground. Cues, however must be created that may also be used when riding. The important part is an understanding of how positive reinforcers work so that they can be created to work for both situations on the ground and in the saddle. Goals and objectives are best organized to promote both behavior on the ground and riding.

In operant conditioning there is a distinction made between primary and secondary reinforcers. Most trainers understand that primary reinforcers deliver a food reward when the behavior is performed. The part that becomes confusing concerns rewards that may effectively be turned into rider cues. This is a basic explanation of how primary and secondary reinforcers work.

Primary reinforcers: A cue, a stimulus or something the trainer does or gives that is reinforcing because it satisfies a biological need. The most common one for horses is food.

Secondary reinforcers: A cue, a stimulus that has been connected or associated with primary reinforcers or some rider cue. This cue is something that has no meaning by itself, but when the cue is consistently repeated at the same time as giving food becomes important to the horse.

The difference between various animals will define the choice primary and secondary reinforcers. Humans have very complicated primary reinforcers consisting of not only food, water, warmth, but include hugging and close contact. Secondary reinforcers are those things that become associated with primary reinforcers. So the human will think primary reinforcer when a "Favorite Hamburger" sign is seen. So in the next step the "Favorite Hamburger" sign becomes a secondary reinforcer because of previous association with food-a primary reinforcer. Our horse friend on the other hand must have this relationship between the primary and secondary reinforcer clearly demonstrated in very basic ways. Trainers often mistakenly assume that the things that reward us are the same for horses; like praise. These symbols only become a reward when they are paired with primary reinforcers like the hamburger sign for us signals food. If a horse is given the same words, in the same tone at the same time with food, and repeated many times the praise words will eventually become a secondary reinforcer. A friend described a situation about a truck that delivered the food to her barn daily. The horses could identify the sound of the truck and knew that the next event was food. Any obvious happening may be paired and become a cue for food. There are many examples like this that occur randomly around our horses like food cans being opened, cars arriving, and doors opening. All we are doing is taking advantage of a learning opportunity and deciding on a cue that may be used later for other performance. Once we decide on a cue it is repeatedly given every time a primary reinforcer is given. After practicing this procedure the cue will stand in for the primary reinforcer, just like the truck's sound signaled food.

4. Examples of Secondary Reinforcers for Rider and Trainer

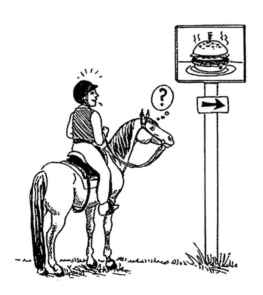

Secondary reinforcer for horse   Secondary reinforcer for rider
Both behaviors are learned

Key Points

- Popular methods of horse training are based on operant conditioning, but not explained in a manner that allows replication.
- The difference between the type of animal (dog, pigeon, duck, horse, etc.) will define different primary and secondary reinforcers.
- Horse behavior on the ground responds well to the creation of secondary reinforcers that are connected with the task-items like bridles, halters and various sounds.
- Operant conditioning makes a distinction between primary and secondary reinforcers.

3. Consequences Using Positive Reinforcers

The Purpose: To understand how **positive reinforcers** can encourage behavior to repeat.

As stated in the last chapter reinforcers are those events that strengthen the response or increase the rate of responding. (Like the arrival of the food truck has the barn of horses responding) On the simplest level rewarding the horse consists of the horse performing a desired behavior and giving the desired reward immediately.

3. Table: Relationship Between Behavior and Rewards

Desired Behavior	Reward or Positive Reinforcers given **immediately** after the behavior - given **every** time until the behavior is secure and learned

This sequence works very satisfactorily especially with tasks that are performed on the ground that are easy to control. Examples would be tasks like: horse comes to the corral gate, stands instead of running away when being turned out, putting on halters and bridles. These are fairly easy to control because they follow the previous model: desired behavior = reward. Think of it in terms of a bonus. Everyone likes to get a bonus for a job well done and tends to repeat the work that received the reward. So if we want Flash to come and put on the halter, the behavior is rewarded every time.

Flash doesn't make the connection unless....

5. Example of a Cue

Give Flash a primary reward when the halter is
shown, and he'll come to the trainer and have it put on.

The halter is presented and a reward is given each time until the behavior is learned. The sight of the halter will then becomes a secondary reinforcer that is a symbol or stands in for the primary reinforcer food. When Flash sees the halter it means a pleasurable happening or reward. No gadgets are necessary. Horses differ from other animals in that all the objects used by the trainer can become a secondary reinforcer.

4. Table: Increase Behavior by Rewarding Immediately After the Behavior

Desired **Behavior** The horse allows the halter to be put on when the trainer shows it to the horse	Reward or **Positive Reinforcer** - Given immediately after the behavior as soon as the horse allows the halter to be put on a reward is given.

Key Points

- Reinforcers are events that strengthen the response or increase the rate of responding.
- A positive reinforcer is another way of saying a reward.
- Everyone likes to get a bonus for a job well done.
- If you want a behavior to reoccur, you create the same situation, using the same cue that was previously rewarded.

Schedules of Reinforcement

Most schedules of reinforcement begin any new behavior by giving the reward every single time to make sure the behavior is learned. The aspect is most important with horses. After the behavior is learned the trainer can move to a variable or intermittent schedule of reinforcement where the horse is rewarded every other time, then every third time, and then randomly. Consider the strong effect of variable schedules of reinforcement. Scientists in labs (Skinner, 1974) have demonstrated the long-term effect of these types of reward schedules. The behavior is remembered for a long period of time. For example a pigeon in a lab, kept repeating a behavior over 10,000 times receiving no reinforcement before the behavior became extinct. It is the reason why gambling is so popular and a very strong behavior.

6. Getting the Payoff

B Goodhorse will keep pulling the arm even though he is only reinforced occasionally because he has been randomly rewarded

Reinforcers Paired with a Stimulus or Cue

Reinforcers become even more useful and practical for training horses when they are assigned to a cue such as an object, recognized place, sound, or touch. The trainer can pick any convenient cue. Preferable are sound and touch that can be used both on the ground and in the saddle. This is an important consideration when picking a cue.

5. Table: Simple Behavior and Reward

Desired **Behavior** Examples of various behaviors that could be rewarded	Reward or **Positive Reinforcer-** given immediately after the behavior
Horse comes to gate	Reward of carrots, horse treat, etc
Horse allows bridle, halter to be put on	Reward
Horse turns around facing the gate and stands quietly for a few seconds	Reward

Important Note: Horses aren't given the reward for any other behavior except the one specified. This includes looking in pockets, hands or other places. This isn't the behavior that's being rewarded. Horses learn easily by chance or random acts if they are rewarded. This is **very strong**-rewards are powerful. Trainers need to consider accurately the behavior to be rewarded and reward **only** that behavior. Rewards aren't bribes. Bribes are incorrect attempts by the trainer to offer the reward **before** the behavior is performed. Timing is critical. Incorrect timing is how the 'old wives tales' originate telling us that horses will learn to bite. Animals are taught to bite by the incorrect use of rewards. If horses are allowed to take rewards from the trainer when they want, the behavior of being aggressive will be reinforced.

7. The Shakedown

"This is a shakedown ...put your hands in the air."

To make it easier to control the desired behaviors, add the stimulus or cue of choice, then immediately give the reward. The easier choice is to pick readily available items to use as the cue or even the item itself as in the case of the halter or bridle. As the behavior is consistently reinforced some item is present like the halter or bridle and automatically becomes the cue or secondary reinforcer. For example if I'm walking around the farm the horses will notice me, but if I go to the gate they all immediately come and line up at the gate. In this case someone standing by the gate is the cue or stimulus that a reward is forth coming. No running around looking for gadgets. The theme on our farm is "Got Carrots™". In the normal routine, allowing sights, sounds, and events that are easily available to become the cue or secondary reinforcer, makes behavior training simple. When trainers continually become a preceding event or the antecedent to a reinforcing event, the person becomes an additional secondary reinforcer for our horses. In other words, people become associated with the primary reinforcers of food and pleasurable happenings, making training much easier.

6. Table: Desired Behavior-Paired with Stimulus/Cue-Reward

Behavior	Stimulus	Contingency
Desired behavior	Cue	Reward or Positive Reinforcing consequence
Horse comes to gate	Cue of choice	Reward
Horse puts on bridle	Sight cue of bridle	Reward
Horse face gate-quiet for turn out. Attentive to trainer-not looking in pockets....	My choice—snap my fingers as soon as they come to attention	Reward

Behavior: Horses go out to one pasture together line up facing the gate waiting patiently and attentively towards trainer until I signal and reward. One of the horses is a 14-month-old colt. All horses are facing the trainer quietly waiting for the cue to walk away. The colt is also being trained for a halter class, routinely he stands quietly waiting for the cue; no whip waving, jerking the halter, or shouting. This is also a very important safety factor and the attention cue can become a routine method of positively handling horses.

Key Points

- Most schedules of reinforcement begin any new behavior by giving the reward every single time to make sure the behavior is learned.
- Training starts with primary reinforcers and moves to secondary reinforcers.
- Reinforcers become even more useful and practical for training horses when they are assigned to a cue such as an object (training whip, halter), sight (trainer), recognized place (gate), sound (snap), or touch (pat-here's where the pat-good horse routine fits).
- To make it easier to control the desired behaviors, we add the stimulus or cue of choice, then immediately give the reward.
- Eventually training moves away from the schedules of primary reinforcers–food
- In the normal routine, allowing sights, sounds, and events that are easily available to the trainer to become the cue, or secondary reinforcer, and makes behavior training easier.
- A safety factor and the attention cue can become a routine method of positively handling horses.

Shaping the Desired Behavior

There are behaviors that aren't natural and don't suddenly or randomly appear. Operant conditioning can take those simple behaviors previously taught and refine them. Skinner describes shaping or refining the desired behavior like a sculptor progressively shapes a lump of clay (Skinner, 1974). It's like making a paper chain and linking each new behavior to a previous behavior. Using a previous example:

7. Table: A Series of Behaviors Chained and Linked Together

Desired **Behavior**	**Stimulus** or Cue	Positive **Reinforcer**
Put on halter	Sight of halter	Carrot or horse treat

Horse putting on halter-Chain of behavior rewarded

Horse stays while halter is put on -Reward (carrot or other horse treat)
Horse makes a motion toward the halter, it is put on -Reward
Horse makes a motion toward halter, touches halter, it is put on-Reward
Horse makes a motion toward halter, pushes nose d own in halter, it is put on-Reward
Horse sees halter, puts head down into halter, it is put on -Reward

Each step asks the horse for a little more and creates the final behavior by rewarding small steps. This is known as **successive approximation**. The halter becomes a sight cue or secondary reinforcer and eventually after enough practice, the trainer produces the halter and the horse will immediately place his head in it. Actually the chain of behavior doesn't have to go to the last step to be successful, but this is a fun activity to practice to become experienced in using the tools and demonstrates the power behind the procedures of operant conditioning.

Key Points

- There are behaviors that aren't natural and aren't voluntarily produced by the horse.
- The tool of shaping rewards the behavior that resembles the response to be learned until the desired behavior is obtained.
- Shaping behavior provides the systematic reinforcement of behavior to bring about more complicated behavior.
- Secondary Reinforcer for horse.

8. Pat-pat: What does it mean?

Pat-Pat only means something
when initially paired with food
The pat-pat then becomes a stand in for food
or a primary reinforcer. Pat-pat has no meaning
for the horse unless this link is made.

So if the pat-pat "Nice Horsy" will mean something, it must be paired explicitly with food. If we perform the cue pat-pat 'good horse' comment every time we feed, this cue will become very strong. The additional secondary reinforcer becomes the person feeding. This explains why horses recognize the person who feeds. By observing your horse, you will identify favorite rewards. Diet constraints will possibly dictate healthy choices. An example of positive reinforcers or rewards is seen in the work of the Spanish Riding School. The work in hand is immediately rewarded with sugar from sacks hidden under their jackets. Obviously the horses aren't being hand rewarded while ridden, but rewarded with less obvious means of secondary reinforcers, like the pat-pat. Because of the nature of riding activities as compared with tricks and work on the ground, rewards from the discipline of riding need to be thought out differently. By thoroughly understanding this simple method of using rewards or positive reinforcers, the trainer can then proceed to the next levels of combining more complicated combinations and reinforcers as discussed in the next chapters. By being aware of this essential aspect, you will approach each task by analyzing the relationship to the horse and what task is to be accomplished and how it is being reinforced or rewarded. Complete understanding of this basic foundation of **operant conditioning,** or how we operate or change behavior will also allow the trainer to retreat and analyze different uses of reinforcement when complicated training ceases to work. Furthermore the trainer has the provision of secondary reinforcers that stand for the tangible reward of food. This is the benefit of understanding the procedures of changing behavior rather than memorizing passed on information.

Key Points

- All three areas are important: Stimulus, Behavior, and Consequence.
- There are other types of reinforcers but positive reinforcers produce and encourage confidence and stability in the partnership.
- Behavior will increase by the use of primary and secondary reinforcers.
- Behavior becomes easier to control when it is created on cues.
- Complete understanding of a basic foundation of operant conditioning, will allow the trainer to retreat and analyze schedules of reinforcement when goals for performing complicated behavior or tasks cease to work. The important part is the ability to look at each step to the behavior and understand how it is increased or decreased.

4. Reinforcers: Tools of the Trade

The Purpose: To understand how negative reinforcers can increase behavior if effectively used.

Behavioral training to be completely effective must correctly use the tools of the trade. A Phillips screwdriver will ruin a plain screw. Incorrect reinforcers will not produce the desired results. Horse training tools of trade for the most part fall into the category of repetitive behavior on the part of riders/trainers with little understanding about why what is being used works. As long as the horse continues to perform no one questions the methods or tools of training. However, later on in the training the incorrect work surfaces when the horse returns from the trainer and demonstrates an aversive attitude toward human partners. Most owners fail to understand or analyze what has happened to change their horse's behavior, or take responsibility for the cause-effect relationship. Many rely on the human models of psychoanalytic psychology. In the case of animals the best tools are those that act on observable behavior rather than seeking underlying problems or emotions. Behavior science and specifically operant conditioning can remedy observable behavior through the systematic use of reinforcers with proper sequence and usage.

As explained in the previous chapters, contingencies are effects or actions immediately following a behavior that will increase or decrease a course of action. Contingencies are large broad groups of all these effects that have the ability to change behavior. To refine the effect, by using positive or negative reinforcers, each reinforcer has its own outcome. Reinforcers are the tools for behavior change.

Key Points

- Behavior science, specifically operant conditioning, can change observable behavior through the systematic use of reinforcers with the proper sequence and usage.
- Reinforcers are the tools for behavior change.

Negative Reinforcers: Not Really Negative

Negative reinforcers aren't really negative but merely increase and strengthen other types of behavior so that the trainers can schedule positive reinforcers or rewards. As previously stated any type of action or behavior that has a consequence (reinforcer) is likely to be repeated. Negative Reinforcers can be used to train the desired behavior but unfortunately are also the ways that most horses learn inappropriate behavior and should be an important consideration for the trainer. B.F. Skinner (1974) describes a negative reinforcer as strengthening any behavior that reduces or terminates it: "when we take off a shoe that is pinching the reduction in pressure is negatively reinforcing and we are more likely to do so again when a shoe pinches" (p. 51). Using Skinner's example there are several examples of daily occurrences that happen by chance because the trainer or rider doesn't understand the critical relationship between behavior and reinforcers in horse training. The effect is outlined in this table.

8. Table: Negative Reinforcers

Stimulus-	Behavior-	Consequence
Signal or some kind of cue present-could be visual, sound, touch....	An action that stops or reduces the effect	An effect or action
Shoe put on the foot and pinches	Take the shoe off	Shoe stop pinching

Key Points

- Negative reinforcers strengthen any behavior that reduces or terminates the unpleasant effect of the negative reinforcer.
- Negative reinforcers are commonly described as rewards-this is inaccurate because the stimulus is unpleasant to the subject-like the pinching shoe.
- Important to delineate the effects of positive reinforcers or rewards and negative reinforcers. Outcomes are very different.

Negative Reinforcers as Useful Training Tools

Negative reinforcers have a powerful effect if understood and correctly used. They allow the trainer to use the tool especially when riding to encourage the horse to complete tasks and learn complicated series of behavior. They also allow the rider to become more positive and reward frequently. Think about the following examples of the use of negative reinforcers that encourage the horse to complete the task. Notice that in the example the trainer ends the chain of behavior using positive reinforcers or rewards.

The most common use of the negative reinforcers occurs with the use of the reins

8. Table: Negative Reinforcer–Use of Reins

Stimulus	Behavior	Consequence
Signal or some kind of cue present -could be visual, sound, touch …	An action that stops or reduces the effect	An effect or action – pressure on the mouth
Reins in contact with the horse's mouth	The horse reduces movement	Reins apply pressure to the mouth and release the pressure as soon as the horse responds

If done correctly the consequence or negative reinforcers **stops immediately** when the horse responds. The second part of this training session is when the horse successfully completes several correct responses a positive reinforcer or a reward is given. See how this would look in the chart below. The more advanced the horse becomes in the chain of behaviors, the longer the intervals between the rewards may become. How many riders or trainers are aware of the critical relationship between the behavior and the type of consequence?

9. Table: Negative and Positive Reinforcer

Stimulus- signal or some kind of cue present-could be visual, sound, smell, touch....	Behavior- an action that stops or reduces the effect/increases or encourages	Consequence–an effect or action
Reins in contact with the horse's mouth apply unpleasant pressure	The horse reduces movement	**Negative Reinforcer-**Reins apply pressure to the mouth **Pressure immediately yielded when the horse responds**
Reins in contact with the horse	The horse completes several correct responses	**Negative Reinforcer** Reins yielded totally
Pat or rub neck- previously taught by pairing with a primary reward	After completing several correct responses	**Secondary reinforcer** previously taught by pairing with primary reinforcers or food rewards
End of session	Dismount	**Primary reinforcer-**food Continually paired with the secondary reinforcer- pat -pat

Many riding books discuss the yielding of the reins, but not why it encourages the horse.

There is a crucial connection between the negative reinforcer and the timing of the release. If the negative reinforcer isn't stopped and timed with the desired behavior, the horse will not make the learning association. This example is certainly a must for the young horse beginning or the horse in retraining. It is also the reason for creating very short chains of behavior in the beginning work.

Key Points

- Negative reinforcers have a powerful effect if understood and correctly used.
- If done correctly the consequence or negative reinforcers stops immediately when the horse responds.
- Negative reinforcers allow the rider to communicate difficult tasks to the horse initially and use positive reinforcers or reward them after completing complex chains.

Negative Reinforcers with Negative Results

Now think about the following examples:

- The horse that initially feels the uncomfortable weight of the saddle placed on his back is suddenly pinched with the girth, and jumps free of the saddle is likely to repeat the action. The horse has reacted to the pinching girth and by the behavior that stopped the pinching by jumping away.

The solution is to make sure the girth doesn't become a negative reinforcer for the behavior of jumping or moving about. Horse training books suggest various techniques such as progressive cinching to preclude such occurrences. What happens if another scenario plays out? Is the relationship to the stimulus, behavior, and contingency understood?

- The horse that is suddenly spurred, bolts losing the rider. For training a professional bronco this works, if not the situation becomes dangerous for any rider with spurs. The spurs now have become the cue for being free of the annoying rider.

One solution is delaying the use spurs until the horse understands an easier task such as moving away from the leg. Understanding the relationship to the stimulus, behavior and contingency allows the trainer other solutions designed for the unique situation. It also allows for scrutiny of horse training books. A quote from "The complete Training of Horse and Rider" (Podhajsky, 1965, p.58) makes an excellent case.

"The spur should be used only in an advance stage of training, and only when required to reinforce the pushing aids. The use of the spur is the last resort and, as with other things in life, the last resort should be reserved for emergencies. The spur should touch the horse's side with an increase pressure of the leg and the application should be discontinued the moment the aid has obtained the required results".

- A horse being mounted moves away from the rider prohibiting the rider from placing weight on the back. The action of weight while mounting the horse is the negative reinforcer increasing the likelihood of the horse moving away.

The solution that many training books provide is having an assistant stand with the horse controlling the behavior so the correct response is practiced. The second scenario that may also occur is that the reins are pulled while mounting, and the horse moves off creating another negative reinforcer pulling the reins, and increasing the horse moving off. Many riders now decide that the reins must be pulled or yanked creating an aversive stimulus or punishment that will be discussed in the next chapter.

Poor understanding and inappropriately applied negative reinforcers are large measure of why horse training is unsuccessful. It ranges from merely mediocre performance to outright dangerous behavior on the part of the horse-human team.

Every training tool if used correctly has the potential for good and, if used improperly, harm. The complete understanding of reinforcers can keep the training out of harm's way by allowing consistent observation of behavior and positively rewarding the behavior desired. Remember our friend the horse can't be biting kicking and standing quietly at the same time. Using the correct reinforcer provides the tools needed to create the desired behavior.

Key Points

- Poor understanding and inappropriately applied negative reinforcers are why some horse training is unsuccessful.
- Using the correct reinforcer can provide the tools needed and give task success.

How Can Negative Reinforcers Help?

Negative reinforcers can help positive training, enhance training, and improve the rider-horse relationship if several concepts are recognized:

1. Pay careful attention to the behavior, the small tasks that are being trained.
2. Attend to random behavior that occurs, often by chance when restraining or preventing behavior.

3. Systemically and correctly use the negative reinforcer to communicate the desired task, paying strict attention to the timing of the reinforcer.

4. Make sure the horse demonstrates the task, and when it is completed make sure it is rewarded.

5. Use a schedule that quickly rewards the desired behavior.

6. Keep in mind the easily remembered definition for negative reinforcers given by B.F. Skinner (1976) as strengthening any behavior that reduces or terminates it: "when we take off a shoe that is pinching the reduction in pressure is negatively reinforcing and we are more likely to do so again when a shoe pinches" (p.51).

5. Aversive Stimulus or Punishment

> *Punishment should never be given in anger because actions committed in anger will later be regretted.*
>
> —Xenophon 400 B.C.

The words aversive and punishment in the context of this chapter will be defined as a consequence or effect that reduces the probability of the behavior. Even though the word "punishment" can mean an aversive sequence, it is used to denote any action that makes an activity cease or behavior stop that will be counter-productive to the horse and future performance. These actions that may become unsociable, as the examples of biting, kicking, and rearing, often cause horses to be poorly treated. Perfectly timed punishment often no more than a loud noise, allows disruptive behavior to be stopped and desirable behavior rewarded.

Punishment can be an effective tool to stop a negative behavior so that a trainer may proceed to a reward situation. The difficulty is that punishment often works very effectively and becomes over used by the trainer. The thought behind this is; if a little works then more is better. In behavioral terms the trainer becomes encouraged, or positively reinforced to use punishment or force because it worked. All of us repeat behavior that works. Finally it is the first and only tool that is used. One of the contrary aspects of only using punishment is that to continue to be effective the intensity must be increased. This often appears true until a certain point and generally at this point it is often too late with horses to renew confidence in the training and the trainer. Because there are certain unforgivable aspects of using aversive stimulus, it's of extreme importance that it is well understood.

To understand the effect of punishment or aversive stimulus let us review the contingencies again: contingencies—effects or actions that will either make something happen or not. Remember the following model? Food is generally associated with rewards because it is strongly desired and with horses associated with survival.

11.Table: Positive Reinforcer or Reward

Behavior	Reward or **Positive Reinforcer** given immediately after the behavior - increases behavior

Now consider undesirable behavior, those actions that should not occur, that are undesired or behaviors to be removed or stopped.

12.Table: Aversive Stimulus-Aversive Control/Punishment

Undesired **Behavior**	**Aversive stimulus** or punishing consequence-given immediately after the behavior-stops, decreases, weakens behavior, or removes it from the repertoire

Example of Aversive Stimulus Properly Used

One explanation of practical usage of an aversive stimulus used for the safety of enclosing horses is the electrically charged fence wire. The horse, immediately upon touching the wire near the fence, is given a small unpleasant shock and stays away from the fence. If you have any doubt that the horse recognizes small stimuli or cues consider the following: a fence is protected with a hot-wire that closes at the gate. The horses will not approach the gate until the wire is taken down. They readily approach the gate and touch the gate easily recognizing the difference between the neutral gate and the aversive hot-wire. This description is one example of how an aversive stimulus or control can provide a positive benefit and keep our partners out of harms way. The other aspect is the cue, which is the fence, isn't associated with the trainer.

9. Example #1: The Fence

10. Example #2: The Nip

It's important to think very carefully about setting up an aversive control environment. Skinner (1975, p.68) states that punishment is often confused with negative reinforcers, but punishing contingencies are just the opposite of reinforcing. Perhaps some of the confusion comes from the common use of the words positive and negative. In this context it is the effect of the reinforcer on the behavior that is described. It's the behavior that we are trying to change when training a horse to do a task. Complete understanding of the tool is central to success. Look again at a chart of the types of contingencies to better understand their use as our operating tools.

13.Table: Contingencies

#1 Positive Reinforcer/Reward	#2 Negative Reinforcer	#3 Aversive stimulus/punishment
Strengthens or Increases the behavior	Strengthens or Increases the behavior that reduces or stops the negative reinforcer	Stops or weakens the behavior or removes behavior that was learned

From the chart it can seen that aversive stimulus/punishment has a very different outcome on behavior than the positive and negative reinforcers. Aversive stimulus stops behavior or removes behavior from the repertoire.

Strong Cautionary Words About Aversive Control

Difficulties arise from the improper and incorrect use and timing of an aversive stimulus. Because of the strength of potential aversive control, it can cause irreparable damage. When improperly timed it can actually encourage undesired behavior. The electric fence is an excellent example of a perfectly timed aversive control because the fence always delivers the shock as the horse touches the forbidden fence. Now if the battery is dead or the electricity is off, the fence will still have the same aversive effect because the lesson has been learned so effectively. It'll take a long time before the horse mistakenly or randomly touches the fence to find no shock. There are very clever horses however that hear the clicking of the fence charger and recognize the cue when the hot wire is aversive. These horses operate on the sound cue rather than the visual cue of the fence explaining the reason for training method failure.

A common mistake for the second example of the biting horse is to punish the horse by striking them. Even if you strike on the shoulder it won't take long for the horse to recognize the swinging hand and move away. If you remember the effect of the negative reinforcer that increases the behavior that precedes it, you will now understand why horses are so good at escaping-they have been reinforced. The cue of the swinging arm is also associated with the trainer. Escape is one of the primary instincts of preservation from predators. This natural instinct is one of the common reasons that most punishment used on horses fail: The horse, using his instinct to run, escape, and get out of harm's way, is reinforced by using these evasive actions. A trainer only has to fail once or maybe twice to reinforce evasive behavior. Failed attempted punishment makes it very hard to remove.

Important Points

Because of the unforgiving nature of punishment it is very important to carefully think about each situation and plan how it will be handled rather than impulsively acting without thought. Again the aversive control is a very strong contingency and may easily change into reinforcing escape behavior. The late Podhajsky, director of the Vienna Spanish Riding School during the time when the beautifully trained white Lippizaner escaped wartime Austria, has some excellent words of caution:

"There is a close relationship between aids, punishment and rewards. Correctly and justly applied they will prove their value as a means of education and will compliment each other in the course of training. The actions of aids and punishments may over-lap because every aid can be increased to the degree of punishment therefore, the different aids should first be carefully considered before resorting to punishment, always remembering that the reward is of greater importance than punishment" (Podhajsky, 1965, p. 54).

Key Points

- Punishment can be an effective tool to stop a undesirable behavior so that a trainer may proceed to a reward situation.
- The difficulty is that punishment often works very effectively and becomes over used by the trainer.
- Because there are certain unforgivable aspects of using punishment, it is of extreme importance that it's well understood.
- Difficulties arise from the improper and incorrect use and timing of punishment. It must always be delivered **immediately**, and timed with the desired behavior.

- If the punishing stimulus or cue is associated with the trainer, it will reduce confidence in the trainer.
- Failed attempts to punish make it very hard to be remove the evasive behavior that follows.
- If the horse becomes aware of his strength and power he will discover he can use it against the rider.

Part Two:

Using Behavior Modification for Training Horses

Introduction: Using Behavior Modification for Training Horses

---

Operant conditioning shapes behavior
as a sculptor shapes a lump of clay

—B.F Skinner

The first part of the book describes the basic principles that allow the trainer to change behavior using the basic three-part contingency of operant conditioning.

14. Table: Review of Stimulus, Behavior and Consequence

Stimulus	Behavior	Consequence

Part II discusses the specific aspects of horse training that differ from other animals that might be trained. Among some of those differences are:

- Philosophy of Horse Training
- The Trainer, the Horse and the Environment
- Survival–Horse Specific Behavior
- Analyzing Horse Training Literature
- Rider Aids and Training Devices
- Additional Horse Training Information

Horses because of their unique personality traits exhibit behaviors different from the other animals that we may have in our lives like dogs, cats, and other pets. If we lived as close to our horses as we do our other pets there would be more similarity to the techniques that are used with animals such as dogs.

Many training methods use natural behavior and so-called instincts to obtain horse training. These methods are useful for work on the ground. They work well as long as the horse provides the behavior. Difficulties arise when the horse no longer provides those responses or never offers them. Just because horses exhibit certain behaviors like following the herd, disciplining each other, grooming, and forming hierarchies and groups doesn't preclude explaining that behavior, reinforcing the part we want, and using it for beginning socialization. Preferable to standing around waiting for a horse to come, is to start cueing and reinforcing the desired behavior.

The following chapters discuss some of the aspects that provide the uniqueness of training horses. All these horse specific behaviors contribute to the training and knowledge permitting the trainer to consider behavior and use it to create an environment and world surrounding horse training.

6. Philosophy of Horse Training

Horses who have bad characters are
rare; generally their vices are the result of
the inexpert handling by riders lacking in
experience.

—Nuno Olivera

As the reader has probably concluded, behavioral horse training
has philosophical implications. It takes a serious commitment to
become knowledgeable to effectively train the horse while still
preserving the contented, cooperative relationship. These implications reflect how the rider/trainer approaches horse training
and the consideration of methods to be used. Does the
rider/trainer seek information and literature that approaches
training by only using the behavior that horses naturally produce? Examples include herding, grooming, flight, curiosity, and
food seeking. If training is limited to natural responses and
behaviors, the training of more complicated behaviors that
occurs while riding are out of reach.

Will the horse training /riding lesson be approached with
fuzzy goals and unclear objectives? Or does the trainer approach
with clear steps of every act or behavior and think of it in terms
of wanting to encourage or discourage that behavior? If you're
trying to learn this method it's produced by gradual sequential
actions on the part of the rider/trainer and not some mysterious
series of actions. Remember behavior and interaction between

the environment occur even if you don't make an active decision to intervene or choose to do anything about it. Behavioral science helps create the response or behavior the horse should perform and doesn't wait for a chance response; hence the name **operant conditioning.**

Good Horse and Bad Horse Philosophy

Trainers must be willing to change their point of view to looking at observable behavior that the horse performs instead of an internal unobservable emotions or feelings. If the trainer views the behavior of the horse as an internal reason, then actions aren't in control by the rider or trainer. If the actions of the horse are viewed as observable events, then these events can by be changed by the tools discussed in Part I of this book. Sound like playing with words? A resounding no. The chart outlines the reasons.

15. Table: Good Horse and Bad Horse

Good horse	Bad horse
Observable behavior can change	Observable behavior can change.
Internal reason behavior can't change	Internal reason behavior can't change It is just a bad horse

Behavior modification from a philosophical point of view observes what is happening and makes an active decision about changing behavior and actively makes those decisions. With horses this philosophy is easy because horses are in our thought-ful, appreciative care. After all we are responsible.

The Horse Trains the Trainer

Consider why trainers persist in their methods or philosophy. Is it because they understand why the training works or the following explanation? Consider the trainers who claim to have successfully trained thousands of horses. Behaviorally how is this explained? Every time the trainer does an action with a horse and the horse performs what is desired the trainer is highly likely to repeat this action or behavior and considers the horse trained. Are the horses that didn't perform the behavior considered trained? If we review the lessons of chapter 2, any behavior that is successful or rewarded is likely to occur and this applies to the trainer just as much as the horse.

16. Table: Trainer Positively Reinforced (Trainer thinks smart trainer)

Stimulus	Behavior	Consequence
The trainer gives some type of aid, signal , or cue	The horse does a desired action	The trainer is "positively reinforced" or rewarded and the behavior will increase

Consider the next explanation. This time the trainer is unsuccessful in getting the horse to perform the desired actions.

17.Table: Trainer "punished" when horse doesn't perform (Trainer thinks stupid horse)

Stimulus	Behavior	Consequence
The trainer gives some aids, signals, or kind of cues	The horse **doesn't** perform the desired behavior	The trainer will continue to try because of previous rewarded behavior - until extinction

When horse training is thought of in these terms it becomes clear that the trainer is a part of this change of attitude. It's not a broad-based ideal of loving horses but a clear definable, observable behavior that results in a friendship/partnership where the partners like each other because of likeable behavior. Horses are hard to like when they're always pushing the trainer around. What begins to happen is that the trainer starts to change his/her attitude to training. Instead of approaching horses with frustration, fear, or even anger and descriptions about the personality of the horse and internal feelings that can't be changed, the trainer recognizes observable trainable behavior. The trainer can't change the horse's behavior until an active decision is made about what behavior needs to be changed. There are implications obvious for any educational training activity whether it's training students to ride, or horses to be ridden. Instead of the rider giving the credit to the horse–"smart horse" and all the blame "stupid horse"–the credit may be shared for the trained behavior. The outcome of using this method is that the trainer/rider begins to change. Yes, in this way the horse does start changing the trainer's behavior because each time the horse is approached for a training session the trainer will consider how his or her actions complete the circle.

11. Mirror mirror....

Your horse is your mirror
— *Old German proverb*

Key Points

- It takes a serious commitment to become knowledgeable to effectively train the horse while still preserving the contented, cooperative relationship.
- If you're trying to learn this method it's produced through gradual sequential actions on the part of the rider/trainer not some mysterious series of actions that can't be logically followed at a later session.

- Every time the trainer does an action with a horse and the horse performs what's desired the trainer is highly likely to repeat this action or behavior.
- Trainers must be willing to change their point of view by looking at observable behavior instead of internal unobservable reasons.

7. The Trainer, Horse, and Environment

> No matter what our philosophy of behavior may be, we are not likely to deny that the world about us is important.
>
> —B. F. Skinner

It works for me, but does it work for you? As often read, much of what trainers do is based on successful repetition and use of the surroundings, as often described as the natural method. The difficulty is to explain how to correct problems when the training doesn't go the desired way. Using behavior modification the trainer begins by asking what behavior increased or decreased, and what happened before the behavior. Part of the key to why the training doesn't work may be occurring in the environment or surroundings. What was occurring in the surrounding area that may have become a cue or stimulus for this behavior?

18. Table: Stimulus and Behavior

Stimulus	Behavior
Someone or something is present	An action or reflexive behavior such As startle or flight occurs

If this behavior produced evasive action allowing escape, the behavior is likely to be reproduced in the future when the same someone or something in the environment (stimulus) is present.

What do we want to happen and what are the steps to make the desired actions happen? How will the environment that includes random occurrences, encourage this?

Use of the Environment

Almost everything of importance that happens to the horse is related to the environment. Horses are keenly aware of what goes on around them. Some horses are especially alert and attentive to what is happening nearby and often in the distance. Being a herd animal their lives depended on paying attention and those that didn't became prey to predators. Much of this behavior is specific to horses. Animals have their own characteristics that limit what may be trained, outside the additional physical characteristics that denote talent for a type of horse training such as racing, jumping or dressage. A fish will never climb a tree; likewise a horse. The animal has physical limits that can be trained and are limited by each animal's own species specific behavior. Most horse training seeks to enhance or replace certain behaviors with those that are taught. In other words, to exchange what is generally called natural tendencies for flight and startle responses, to those cues that respond unconditionally to the trainer. In most environments created for training, the horse will respond and then again in others not. The aim of behavioral management is to shape cues that override those reflexive behaviors such as startle and flight, and use the environment to support those actions.

Consider the following example, a manmade environment for encouraging beginning horse training, by using the controlled space of an enclosed arena or fenced in area. The designed environment helps shape the behavior of the horse by directing his actions along a wall. The environment encourages the correct response or behavior desired. In the case of the longe work the correct beginning aids are established such as going forward and being restrained on a cue. The environment limits the movements of the horse until the aids or cues are practiced correctly and learned. An example of this is teaching a young horse to longe using the restrictions of the environment, such as an enclosed space, to teach the aids or cues. The environment helps place the horse in the desired position by limiting the movements. These movements or behaviors are then trained on cue by using reinforcers to become part of a chain of behaviors, used to make beginning training safer and pleasurable for both partners.

It's the responsibility of the trainer to plan the sequence of the behavior that is desired and secure the environment that encourages the actions of the horse. This means that every behavior, such as loading horses into trailers, introducing new objects, work on the ground, and riding lessons need to be thought out with a clear understanding of how the environment will help or hinder the learning process. An example of creating a safe environment is exemplified by the loading procedures used by many airlines to load horses prior to flights. When we arrived to ship horses at the Lufthansa hanger in Germany, a very quiet corner was set aside with chutes that brought the horses right into the containers. There was no apprehension on the part of the horses; the environment encouraged the correct response. The other factor was that all of the horses had positive past experiences with trailer procedures.

When the trainer considers creating any learning environment, it's certain that circumstances will encourage that the likelihood of the desired response occurs. Young horses (or older horses in retraining) started in training are given their first lessons in a quiet, distraction free setting so they initially learn the correct response. Correct responses are easier to maintain than correcting poor behavior. Every beginning training session should consider the preparation of the surrounding area and ensure that it encourages correct behavior. This environment helps the horse focus attention on the training and the tasks at hand. I trained stallions in an outdoor arena that was surrounded with pastures of mares, but this isn't how the work was begun. The work was started in a small enclosed training arena and as the horses successfully progressed, they were moved to more distracting environments gradually.

Identifying Environmental Objectives

The next step is to cue and positively reinforce correct responses; meaning the use of primary and secondary reinforcers as described in Part I. Any type of cue or single behavior may be exchanged and put in place of the ones identified in the examples described in part I. The important aspect is that the horse understands the cue, including eventually used secondary reinforcers, and the environment that supports the sequence. An example of using the environment for creating the correct response for two examples of possible cues would be the following:

Goal: To train a young horse to walk along quietly next to the trainer, using the environment (the wall) to help support and create the desired behavior.

Objective 1: To follow a sight cue of the end of the training whip (trainers who primarily handle horses on the ground may prefer this cue). Using the wall of a quiet, distraction-free enclosed environment, the horse has visual reference of the wall for the behavior.

Objective 2: To move forward on a voice command (my preference is for this cue because it will become a cue for behavior used in riding). Using the wall of a quiet, distraction free enclosed environment, the horse has a visual reference of the wall for the behavior.

Objective 1: Steps of chaining the behavior

• The cue is to follow the end of the training whip
• The whip is held in front of the horse as soon as the horse moves his head toward the end of the whip; a primary reinforcer (reward) is given
• Repeat until learned
• The whip is held slightly out of reach, so the horse must move forwards to reach the end of the whip, a primary reinforcer is given.
• Repeat until learned
• The whip is held out of reach so the horse must move forward several steps to reach the end of the whip, a primary reinforcer is given now paired with a secondary reinforcer of choice (the "pat -pat" can be use here)
• Repeat until behavior is 100% learned before moving to intermittent schedule of reinforcement and adding more steps and eventually moving at the trot.

Objective 2: Steps of chaining the behavior

• The cue is upon hearing the sound from the trainer the horse moves forward
• The sound cue is given and the horse is moved a step forwards; a primary reinforcer (reward) is given
• Repeat until learned
• The sound cue is given and the horse is moved several steps forward; a primary reinforcer (reward) is given
• Repeat until learned
• The sound cue is given and the horse is moved several steps forwards; a primary reinforcer (reward) is given now paired with a secondary reinforcer of choice (the "pat - pat" can be use here)
• Repeat until behavior is 100% learned before moving to intermittent schedule of reinforcement and adding more steps and eventually moving at the trot.

Important Note: Many trainers use a whip to create the behavior of moving forward and sometimes create a horse that is afraid of the whip instead of respecting it as a learned cue for a desired response. Correctly used the whip is a negative reinforcer; increasing moving forwards. Remember any unpleasant like poor use of the whip-that is paired with a response-jumping away event by the horse could become learned behavior (in other words if you use a whip it is possible the same behavior of jumping away may repeat). The whip can be carefully used and exactly timed to assist the response for some horses as a negative reinforcer that is immediately followed by the primary reinforcer that is outlined in the previous objectives (outlined in Part I, Chapter 4).

The environment in these examples is used to limit or control the type of response from the horse. Using an atmosphere of minimum distractions allows the trainer to obtain the correct response. The wall acts as a barrier to direct the movement. An example of a counter productive environment is exemplified in this situation. While training horses in Germany I rode in an arena that had a small hidden opening along the wall where people could look into the hall. These faces that suddenly popped up in the wall and just as suddenly disappeared were a distraction to younger horses. This type of sudden happening, especially in beginning training, paired with an undesired response by the horses, accounts for many unreasonable behaviors learned by horses. Most undesired horse behavior is learned by evasive behavior that increased right after an unpleasant happening either from the trainer or the environment. The trainer wants a horse to eventually become accustomed to distractions in the environment, but in a systematic controlled way. Allowing an unpleasant happening or stimulus to enter into beginning training prematurely should be guarded against. When a learning environment is created, essential considerations for the trainer are:

- Create a learning environment that supports the desired behavior or makes it likely to happen.

- Insure that the surrounding things in the environment doesn't enter or intervene at a time that will be an unpleasant happening, becoming an aversive stimulus-creating a cue for the unpleasant person or thing.

- Use extreme caution when using negative reinforcers or aversive control that could become cued or stimulus paired with the environment, person and objects (like horse trailers, stalls, wash racks, hands, whips, etc.).

Key Points

- Every beginning training session should consider the preparation of the surrounding area and ensure that it encourages correct behavior.
- The environment is used to limit or control the type of response from the horse.
- It is the responsibility of the trainer to plan the sequence of the behavior that is desired and secure the environment that encourages this behavior.
- The important aspect is that the horse demonstrates the cue including eventually used secondary reinforcers, and the environment supports the sequence.

8. Survival and Horse Specific Behavior

> The horse clings to his habits more than any other living creature
>
> —Podhajsky

Don't wait for your horse to give you behavior you want....
Cue it
Reinforce it
Shape it

Just because your horse follows you around in a small enclosure doesn't mean he'll perform this behavior again or in another environment unless...

The basis of much horse behavior is based on survival. All living animals must survive. Each animal develops species specific behavior that supports survival of the animal. At the base of this survival is the need for food. One of the major influences on a foal's life is the mother that provides food.

19. Table: Survival Behavior

Stimulus	Behavior
mare	Suckling = reflexive response foal behavior

Operant conditioning make decisions about the cues to be used, behavior desired, and the reinforcers.

20. Table: Operant Conditioning

Stimulus/Cue	Behavior=operated and decided by the trainer	Consequence
Snap Fingers	Foal seeking trainer	Food=primary reinforcer

Many training programs promote what are called natural training methods. These methods allow the trainer to work with many behaviors that are reflexive reactions and don't strengthen the behavior to consistently repeat. If classical and operant conditioning are understood, not only can the trainer train reflexive reactions and train it on stimulus or cue, but other behaviors that aren't natural may also be trained. Also the behavior is strengthened so it will occur on cue. Additionally the trainer will take great care to insure that reflexive reactions don't become conditioned to a cue, especially in working with young horses that are untrained. It's important to guard against a random happening that enters during a training session and becomes a cue for an unpleasant happening or an **antecedent stimulus** to this unpleasant event.

Imprinting

Konrad Lorenz, an Austrian-German, who studied the behavior of animals, made an important contribution to the study of imprinting. The famous study that was performed with ducklings, became a definitive work about imprinting. The natural instinct of ducklings is different than other animals, but still provides information about species specific behavior that can be used by the trainer. Just because ducklings follow the first objects they see doesn't mean this behavior is the same for other animals.

Recent articles published about imprinting give suggestions about becoming part of the foal's beginning environment. Most articles only describe handling the foal. If the previous examples of classical and operant conditioning are used, imprinting the foal's behavior becomes more than forcing the trainer's contact on the foal by handling, but by pairing involuntary, reflexive behavior positively with the trainer. An additional consideration is training the mare to respond to the trainer. In an informal study of 25 mares that were raised together in a pasture, five mares had been previously trained and had close contact with their trainers. The other mares were only used for breeding and hadn't had any extensive contact with trainers and not ridden. All the mares in the pasture had foals. The mares that had been previously ridden and trained brought their foals to their trainers and visitors. Those mares that hadn't been ridden or handled stayed aloof and moved away when visitors approached. It appears that there are other factors involved other than just contact with the foal. Additionally it seems that the behavior of the mare including the amount of training, will play a part in foal behavior. Even more important is to assure that contact with people is pleasurable and that contact increases sociable behavior. Remember people can become a cue for pleasant or unpleasant responses. Cues are neutral until conditioned by a pleasant or unpleasant association.

Animal Play and Horse Specific Behavior

Among the animals there is a variety of what is generally called natural instincts used to describe behavior that isn't taught. In studies about animal play of predatory and non-predatory play behavior, some of the observable differences are described. Predators exhibit certain play in contrast to non-predatory play. Young animals spend much of their time practicing these play behaviors for life survival. In the examples of non-predatory animals much of the play observed is designed to run and flee predators (M. Bekoff, J. A Byers, 1998). These non-predatory play behaviors demonstrate some of the specific behavior that is common to horses. Beginning horse training should consider the aspects of horse specific behavior. Most of what is done to train a young horse is overcoming the behavior of a startle response (commonly called shying) and flight. The animal play explanation of non-predatory animals, such as horses, to flee under stressful, aggressive actions and unknown objects should be considered by trainers. These behaviors are the actions that are unique to training horses, and form the basis from which to work.

Horse Behavior a Snap Using Reinforcers

Operant conditioning provides the means to replace undesired behavior with other forms of behavior. Old cues can be replaced with new cues that obtain desirable responses Instead of waiting for the horse to give the desired response, behavior modification can immediately begin to shape the behavior the trainer wants from a young horse. It's not necessary to wait for the horse to provide voluntary often called natural behavior. If we are in a small environment with a horse we don't have to wait until he decides to approach the trainer. Within the few minutes it takes to give several primary rewards, combined with a cue, the trainer can have a horse approaching and seeking trainer attention. This may then be cued to the secondary reinforcer that now tells the horse every time this cue or stimulus is presented (a sound, sight, or touch) a reward is signaled. The trainer has now actively cued the desired behavior. Want your horse to come and pay attention to you anytime? Reinforce it.

This table reviews how the trainer can train behavior to a cue, instead of waiting for it to be offered.

21.Table: Creating a Cue

Stimulus	Behavior	Consequence
Snap fingers, whistle or other obvious cue	Horse approaches and attends to trainer	Primary reward=food

Note: For this behavior I like to use the snap of fingers because I always have them with me-no need to run and find gadgets. This has paid off in many difficult panic situations. An example of this occurred when I accidentally dropped a lead line and my young colt was free. I snapped my fingers and he immediately came and stood in front of me attentively waiting.

Another important factor is learned with this taught behavior. The snap, whistle or whatever cue becomes a secondary reinforcer, (a cue or stimulus that stands for a reward) but the trainer also becomes a secondary reinforcer, a visual stimulus or cue that stands for a reward. This is a very valuable association to create; a positive relationship with your horse. The string of behaviors follows:

Goal: The horse will approach and attend to the trainer.

Objectives:

1. Every time the horse approaches the trainer, the trainer snaps fingers and rewards (remember this is done every time until the horse performs the behavior).

2. Every time the horse approaches the trainer waits a few seconds, the trainer snaps fingers and rewards (Important not to wait longer than the horse will stand attentively. The horse should perform the correct behavior before the reward).

3. Every time the horse approaches the trainer the trainer waits a little longer (make sure it isn't longer than the horse will perform). As this is practiced the wait may be extended as long as the horse continues to perform the behavior, snap the fingers and reward.

Second step

Goal: The horse will approach and attend to the trainer each time the fingers are snapped. This creates the stand in for the reward and the secondary reinforcer is taught.

1. Every time the trainer snaps the horse approaches and attends and receives a primary reinforcer (**remember not one small motion towards taking anything from the hand is rewarded. This is very important**).

2. This is done every time and then a variable schedule as previously described is implemented.

22. Table: Pick up Feet on Cue.

Stimulus	Behavior	Consequence
Tap leg	Horse picks up feet	Primary reinforcer-food

Goal: To have horse pick up feet on cue

Objectives:

1. Tap the leg and pick up hoof and reward
2. Tap the leg and wait for any movement picking the hoof up and reward
3. Tap the leg and wait for a defined motion of picking up hoof and reward
4. Tap the leg and wait for a more defined motion of picking up hoof and reward
5. Tap the leg and wait for the hoof to be picked up and reward

After the behavior is 100% established change the reward schedule to an intermittent schedule as previously outlined.

How Aversive Actions May Enter the Beginning Training

If a positive reinforcer is timed to a behavior it can increase the behavior's reoccurrence, then conversely an aversive control or inadvertent punishment timed with a behavior, or reflexive response may cause problems with the desired training. Classical conditioning occurs when an **antecedent stimulus** (an event precedes) is presented and timed with a behavior. If the antecedent or preceding event is a positive reinforcer, primary food, there will likely be a positive learning experience that contributes to training. However, if a punishing or aversive effect is the antecedent to the behavior there could be an undesirable training effect. These random antecedent punishing occurrences account for the reason many horses demonstrate what seems to be unexplainable behavior. Often a horse, with a past history unknown to the present owner, exhibits unexplainable reactions to various cues or stimuli that are the results of negative antecedent behavior. The attempt is to explain these behaviors in human psychological terms, when they are actually a reaction to a cue that has been paired with someone or something present during an aversive or unpleasant occurrence.

These descriptions of horse behavior that are based on human behavior and the human psychological model are internal and don't allow for intervention. Horses have a different set of animal specific behaviors. They're feeling animals but don't internalize those feelings. Most of the emotional descriptions given to horses in human psychological terms are rather examples of aversive conditioning when a punishing action has been applied by a trainer. These actions or consequences have been the randomly or the intended cause or antecedent of something that happened to the horse. Whenever the person or thing that closely represents the original cause is presented, the original response of the horse will occur. This behavior will occur in the future when the person or thing (stimulus), is presented even though the original reason is no longer present. This response can also be conditioned in humans and the explanation for why some humans don't like animals, and also why some horses don't like some people.

12. Horse Emotions: If horses offered their emotions...

"I had a difficult childhood, my mother was taken from me when I was very young and my father ran around..."

Most difficulties and undesired horse behavior that is observed isn't the results of an emotional trauma in the human psychological sense but trainer abuse of aversive control. These aversive and extreme punishing contingencies come back to haunt the trainer because the trainer often represents and has become paired with the unpleasant-ill-timed event. The obvious example is a horse that flinches anytime the trainer moves around the horse. It is extremely important to think about and carefully use any aversive control.

Key Points

- Pair all feeding (primary reinforcer) with the trainer-creating a secondary reinforcer =the trainer
- Pair secondary reinforcers with primary reinforcers immediately when beginning training-do the pat-pat and talking while feeding.
- Encourage foal training by not only handling the foal in a positive environment, but by also training the mare.
- Extreme caution to prevent a random punishing antecedent occurrence during training, especially when beginning with young foals and horses. Most of the traumatic happenings to horses happened because of this sequence. Trainers need to be alert for this chain of events.
- To continue a positive approach to training horses, trainers must be alert to those events that may be aversive that precede or are antecedent to training.
- It is extremely important to think about and carefully use any aversive control.

9. Analyzing the Horse Training Literature

All sciences have principles and rules,
by means of which one makes discoveries
leading to their perfection.

Guérinière

In seeking literature to improve horse training, readers should look for information that can help bridge the gap of their present knowledge to expanded competency. To become competent in any area of knowledge there is a body of content. To learn the body of content the material should be separated into sequential steps making it easier to learn. This means the literature is developmentally sound. Skills to be trained are described sequentially in the order of physical ability and level of difficulty for the horse (rider also). Our own beginning school education started with easy tasks that were developed sequentially in difficulty. When we pick literature to help learn any new skill we look for literature that effectively teaches by bridging the gap of what is known to a higher level of proficiency. So it should be with horses. The literature should help bridge the gap between what the horse trainer presently knows and the information to increase this knowledge.

History

History plays a large role in the training of horses and the literature. Much of this history and horse training literature is directed to the working horse necessary for wars, working herds of animals, and pulling vehicles. Some horse training literature is still based in the past history of horse training, including myths, and rumor that fails to consider modern scientific discovery and recreational horse training goals. Even the proponents of less violent methods of horse training fail to use the scientific methods proven successful in creating a positive training environment for animals. A significant amount of the literature is still based in violent methods that make no more sense than "this has always been done", it's a "natural way" or relies on giving the horse the same emotional, feeling thinking process of humans. Horses aren't better or worse in their differences from humans or other animals just diverse and species specific in their behavior.

Many of the oldest training and riding methods practiced by the equestrian masters of the 17th century, observed the necessity for kind but firm training for the highly prized horse used in the art forms of several established riding schools of the period. The doctrines, principles, and the teachings of these masters are maintained by the Spanish Riding School, The French academy of Versailles created in 1680, now know as the Saumur, the German school at Hanover descended from the older academy of Gottingen, (Gianoli, 1969, p.137). Unfortunately, the latter two didn't have the benefit of Walt Disney to promote their fame to film.

With any learning environment the teacher must have an understanding of what is to be taught. By looking at the literature of horse training the reader may find certain periods that were focused on a more violent quick end result. And then again, there were other times in history that had a more enlightened focus of training horses.

These main corner stones of classical training laid some of principles that may be used by today's trainer. Historically this training goes back to the ancient times of Xenophon 400 BC in Greece and provides great insight into many aspects of the horse including horse specific behavior in the natural environment. A student of horse literature with an understanding of behavioral science may read between the lines and include the behavioral context and explanations. This chapter highlights a few excellent considerations about possible training goals and objectives Hopefully the reader will think about what has been read and future reading in a behavioral context, using these choices for training objectives. As mentioned in the beginning, behavioral science is a neutral tool-it is the trainer that will make the value judgments and decide what is in the best interest of the horse. In most educational settings this is the most critical element-to decide what to teach.

Finding Goals and Objectives in the Literature

As we discussed in the first chapter specific goals allow the rider to define the exact behavior and focus on how that behavior can be enhanced. Broad based goals as defined in most books are fine to create a general philosophy about horsemanship but do little to help the trainer to focus on the task or specific behavior. A satisfactory overall goal for horse training could state: schooling an obedient and calm horse. What are the steps to achieve this?

Horsemanship literature often gives several broad based goals. The important goal statement most often doesn't lead to the specifics of the next steps that are the successive behavior or actions that the horse is to perform. Many such books talk about physical development of the horse and repetitious determination necessary for training. General statements about submission of the horse in learning the movements and being generously rewarded are made. The reader is left to decide what the generous rewards are and how they are given.

Translated in behavioral terms this statement means, that we are sure the horse can physically perform the task and has demonstrated one small act. The rider using a primary reinforcer then rewards this demonstrated behavior. Later this behavior is paired with secondary reinforcer. Remember the "pat reward" is really a reward understood by the horse because it has been previously established by pairing it with food. Additionally easing the contact with the mouth, timing this with the "reward pat" will further reward the behavior. The stimulus, the pat, was always previously given with some food, so the pat "stands in" in the horse's mind for the food. Otherwise the pat has no significance at all. I'm sure that if your boss merely gave you a pat at the end of the week you would find another job. How many of you would work for peanuts?

13. Working for Peanuts

Most of us would quit this job

Using the jumping model outlined in behavioral training would follow this step-by-step break down of the broad goal of the horse jumping a two-foot jump.

Goal: horse jumping a two-foot fence

1. The horse is able to perform a trot willingly carrying the rider.
2. The horse will walk over a pole on the ground.
3. The horse will trot over a pole on the ground
4. The horse will trot over a cavalletti raised to the first level
5 The horse continues successfully over poles raise progressively until the goal is reached and then repeated at all of the steps at the canter.

Anytime the horse has difficulty the rider goes back to the previous level. The main focus of this example is the behavioral training many of the particulars may be found in the book "Cavalletti" by the late Klimke. "Work over Cavaletti makes the basic training of *all* riding horses easier. They give the opportunity too, of overcoming more quickly and easily, difficulties in the special arts of jumping, dressage and cross-county" (Klimke, 1969, p.15).

One of my favorite writers is Podhajsky, because he frequently gives excellent examples of the use of behavioral training and also writes sequential statements about the art of riding including longeing, rider position, and the use of aids. An example of this is found in " The Riding Teacher". "The pupil, rewards his horse by patting him and giving him sugar and leads him back to the stable...."(Podhajsky 1974, p.50). Clearly identified is that the primary or food reinforcement is paired with the secondary reinforcers the pat. "In his eagerness to obtain progress the teacher might forget that these periods of rest and reward are necessary to prevent the horse and rider form becoming stale and listless." When the videos of the Spanish Riding School demonstrate the correct use of the reward; the sugar is given, then the pat. In addition it should be added that the rest/reward would be given for the best work for either horse or rider in a lesson.

As the reader considers this theme it is noted that most books don't address rewards or punishment in the index or table of content. Most of the time these themes are entwined in the content of the horse training leaving the reader to recognize the importance to the training. An example of cautionary use of the aids is found in the "School of Horsemanship" by de la Guérinière "if the aids are used wisely and discreetly as they should be with young horses; the lack of care in the beginning is the cause of most vices and disorders into which the horse subsequently falls". In other words horses that are inappropriately rewarded or punished for carelessly picked objectives, run the risk of failure.

If the literature mentions rewards, often they aren't discussed in specific terms, but imprecise generalities. The other confusion is to discuss the negative reinforcer as a reward. This error leads to the incorrect use of both tools. Often we read reports that discuss training principles as asking the horse for that challenge the horse and are less comfortable during the process. The process of letting the horse have release from discomfort is described as a reward. This confusion of rewards, negative reinforcers, and aversive control makes it difficult to train riders to use the best tool. The reason expert trainers are successful is that they understand the effect of the negative reinforcer even though they say they're giving a reward. The trainer releases the uncomfortable aid immediately when the horse performs. Also understood is the exact sequential actions that are needed to move to the next step. The trainer is trained by past successful (or unsuccessful) experiences, of what works and what doesn't (what has or hasn't been reinforced). By not being able to understand or analyze the process, the effect of the trainer is lost.

23. Table: Rider Aids Reinforced

Cue **Stimulus**/Rider Aid	Behavior	Consequence
The rider uses certain aids and the horse performs	The rider will continue to use those same aids because they seemed to work.	Positive reinforcer - increased the behavior of the rider to repeat these aids -because they seemed to get results.

What happens if rider doesn't succeed with those aids?

24. Table: Unsuccessful rider aids continued

Cue **Stimulus**/Rider Aid	Behavior	Consequence
The rider uses certain aids that were previously successful and the horse doesn't perform	The rider will continue to use the same aids because they worked before	The rider was previously reinforced for the using the rider aids- like any behavior reinforced there will be a period before extinction occurs

Key Points

- When we pick literature to help learn any new skill we look for literature that teaches effectively by bridging the gap of what is known to a higher level of proficiency.
- Hopefully the reader will think about what has been read and future reading in behavioral context.

10. Rider Aids and Devices

*It was profound thought that through
the ages has given the name "aids" to the
communication from rider to horse, for
the rider should help his horse to understand him*

—Podhajsky

Tools of the Trade: Rider Aids

There is much discussion in magazines and other literature about the use of certain rider's aids and equipment. As anyone looks at the training books, articles written, and observes riders, it is obvious that there are many tools used in the training of horses. Some of these tools however delicately handled would never fall into the category of humane. These are somewhat apparent, especially when we analyze the effect on the horse and behavior. There are other devices that fall into a neutral area, depending on use. These aids are the generally seen in an array in bits, spurs, whips, and head tying devices.

If the subject is viewed in behavioral terms most of what is used by riders is a tool. As previously discussed, tools are neutral devices that only take on a positive or negative connotation when applied by the rider. It is through the patient, thorough understanding of the effects of the aids, that the rider can use them to obtain willing performance. The focus in this chapter is to look at some of these devices with a behavioral microscope.

The Rider Knows How to Use the Aids

In reviewing the concepts of Part I, tools such as aids and devices are merely to effect a change in the behavior of the horse so the desired behavior is understood and communicated to the horse. The importance of these aids or cues for desired behavior is what happens after the cue. Is behavior increased or decreased? If the aid is used correctly it will get the desired effect. Often the trainer will persist in using an aid that repeatedly fails to produce the desired effect. In many cases the opposite results was produced. As we look at an aid in behavioral terms, the focusing question is, will it increase or decrease the objective desired. Some of the following common riders aids are discussed in behavioral terms in the following explanations and charts. Remember the rider or trainer aid is the means to communicate with the horse what is desired. For communication to be complete it must be understood. In behavioral terms the rider aid is the cue or stimulus. Reviewing our original chart from Part I will allow us to analyze each aid for the desired result on horse training.

25. Table: Review of Important Parts of Operant Conditioning

Cue or stimulus	Desired behavior	Consequence
Rider aids are the actions or cues that communicate with the horse	What is the action or response of the horse	Applied contingencies used to urge or persuade the action desired increase response
Whip	Horse moves forwards	Negative reinforcer
Spurs	Horse moves forwards; moves away from the leg	Negative reinforcer
Legs	Horse moves forward	Negative reinforcer
Bits	Horse yields to contact	Negative reinforcer
Rein devices	Horse yields to pressure	Negative reinforcer

As the reader has noticed most rider aids are negative rein-forcers. The confusion for riders is that they don't understand that releasing or stopping an aid is **not** a reward.

To review the negative reinforcer the chart from Part I follows:

26. Table: Negative Reinforcer

Cue or Stimulus - signal or some kind of cue present-could be visual, sound, smell, touch. ...	Behavior- an action that Stops or reduces the effect	Consequence –an effect or action that increases behavior
Reins in contact with the horse's mouth	The horse reduces movement	Reins decrease pressure to the mouth –removal of the unpleasant stimulus

In review, it is noted that negative reinforcers only continue to work when they stop **immediately** upon the response of the horse.

The choice of the type of aid (rider terms for cue or stimulus) will help the response that occurs and encourage the desired action. If we look carefully at the desired behavior that the aid encourages, it will be noted that some rider aids fail to obtain this result. Many articles are written lamenting the use of certain type of rider aids. These articles often miss the point of what the aid seeks to accomplish and only discuss the failure of the rider using the device. This failure is rider misuse or improper choice of the aid. The focus should be what is the objective of the lesson and how well does the aid or device communicate this to the horse

The following questions should be asked about aids and devices:

- Does the aid or device increase the rate of response or desired behavior?
- Does the rider stop using the device when the horse responds or does the device release the stimulus or cue action after the horse responds?

- Is the device no longer needed after a reasonable time that the horse has learned the desired behavior?
- Does the rider continue to use the device or aid because the horse hasn't learned the correct behavior?
- Will the horse only perform the work with the device or constant use of the aid?

Those aids or devices that fall into a training aid category that continued to be used after the reasonable training period, fail the test of producing the desired horse response or behavior. Some of the devices that fall into this group are those that artificially restrain the horse's position with no release on the correct response of the horse. Examples are the devices that are used to tie the horse's head in a fixed fashion or bits and bridles that allow no yielding response.

- If the rider aids or devices fail the scrutiny of the following sequence: rider aid, horse responds with the desired action, and the aid is stopped; consider:
- Incorrect choice of aid or device for the behavior being taught
- Incorrect use of aid or device.
- Faulty aid or device
- Incorrect use of timing of aid or device

Here lies the fault of most riders' devices from bits to nose chains, and from martingales to cambons, the improper use of a neutral tool. It can't be overly stressed that to pick and use any training device effectively the following must be clearly addressed:

- Objective-What is the single action that the horse should perform?
- Aid-How does this aid or device encourage the desired action?
- Will the aid or device increase and encourage the desired behavior?

The reader will notice that most of the examples of rider aids are negative reinforcers. If the riding experience will continue to be a positive, the rider must consider the use of the negative reinforcer and timely use of a positive reinforcer. In other words depending on the level of training and how far the horse is advanced in the skill, the rider will gage the lesson on these facts. For example of the rider is teaching the halt the progression might looks like this:

Goal: The horse will perform a halt on the desired cue

Objectives:

- On the ground, the horse stops from a walk when hearing a sound.
- On the ground, the horse stops from a walk when hearing a sound and paired with the restraining longe line.
- In the saddle, the horse stops from a walk when hearing a sound paired with the restraining rein.
- Lessons ends on successful completion of task

27. Table: Schedule of Reinforcers

Stimulus or Rider Aid	Behavior	Consequence
1.lSound Cue	Horse stops	Positive Reinforcers Food Tidbit-both primary and secondary reinforcers
Sound cue paired with restraining longe used together	Horse stops	Negative Reinforcer
Sound cue paired with Restraining rein used together	Horse stops	Negative Reinforcer
Pat horse – Praise paired and given with food reward Drop contact Get off Horse Take horse to barn or pasture	End lesson on successful completion of task	Positive Reinforcers- Food reward -both primary and secondary reinforcers

This gives the riders an example of the lesson that is planned with attention to the behavior and how the behavior is to be encouraged through the use of behavioral tools. The lesson would continue with the same outline. Progressing through the gaits as the horse is totally successful at the previous level. The rider may include any extra steps that are needed for individual needs. Some of those might be:

1. Young horses
2. Horses with athletic or balance difficulties
3. Horses in retraining

The lesson also ends within a reasonable time and the riders resist the temptation to continue training after the horse has completed the behavior successfully. If the horse fails to complete the next level during a reasonable amount of time the rider returns to the previous level that the horse can complete successfully. It is very important that the horse end the lesson on the best performance possible at this stage of training. Behavior practiced incorrectly will be remembered just as much as the correct behavior.

Key Points

- Tools such as aids and devices are merely to effect a change in the behavior of the horse so the desired behavior is understood and communicated to the horse.
- The choice of the type of aid (rider terms for cue or stimulus) will help the response that occurs and encourage the desired action.
- Connect cues and aids with primary reinforcers-any cue then becomes a secondary reinforcer.
- Horses are cued or given secondary reinforcement if the cue is something commonly used.

11. Additional Information and Explanations

Equestrian art is the perfect understanding between the rider and his horse.

—Oliveira

Although the principles outlined in part I are easily mastered and can help in obtaining a high success rate with training, additional information adds extra explanations that will increase their effectiveness. The more familiar the reader becomes with using the basic tools of behavior analysis the easier the process becomes. It is suggested that the simple, easier-to-manage process of the following sequence is practiced with some simple task before adding more difficult combinations.

28. Table: Important Parts of Operant Conditioning

Stimulus	Behavior	Consequence

The learning progression will be the same for the trainer as it was for the horse. There is a sequential process that allows learning of each skill before going on to more difficult tasks. The learning sequence for the trainer might follow the example outlined as:

Goal: To become knowledgeable about the skills of behavior modifiction for the purposes of training horses to perform a single task.

Objectives:

- Identify one task for the horse to perform.
- Identify a cue or stimulus to be used for that performance.
- Identify and give a food reward or primary reinforcer each time the horse performs the task.
- Repeat the items 1, 2, 3, of the sequence until learned, rewarding continuously.
- Repeat the items 1,2,3, of the sequence, rewarding intermittently

An easy example to begin familiarizing the trainer with behavioral techniques (Chapter 3, Part I) would be the task of having the horse come to the fence given a cue or put halters on when given a cue. As previously mentioned when the trainer successfully completes a training task, the trainer's behavior is also reinforced. The consequence is on an intangible level or secondary reinforcement but reinforced the same. There are important effects when using reinforcers of a primary or secondary type. Understanding the impact of those differences may mean better results. These results are important when working with horses and one of the frequent reasons that trainers think that a horse has been rewarded when in fact there is no reward. Since most of us are reinforced by secondary reinforcers there is an incorrect assumption that this is the same for our companions the horse. Here is a brief review of primary and secondary reinforcers.

Primary reinforcers are stimulus events that are inherently reinforcing because they satisfy a biological need (Weiten 1989, p.205)

Secondary reinforcers or conditioned reinforcers are stimulus events that acquire reinforcing qualities by being associated with primary reinforcers. In the case of humans most reinforcers fall into the secondary category. They are items that depend on previous learning. Some examples would be praise, flattery, success, and attention from others. A chart of primary and secondary reinforcers for the trainer and .(See notes for additional information).

29. Table: Primary and Secondary Reinforcers

	Stimulus	Behavior	Consequence
Horse	Whistle	Horse comes	Primary reinforcers=carrots
Trainer	Horse Performs desired task	Trainer will repeat actions that influenced the horse to perform	Secondary reinforcer= Success, attention from other trainers,

The significance of this is that unless the connection of the secondary reinforcer is made clear to the horse it isn't a reward. This is why the "good horse" or "pat-pat" on the shoulder means absolutely nothing to the horse-unless it was conditioned with a primary reinforcer. All this means that if you want the "pat-pat" to mean anything it must be done while giving a primary reinforcer. Horses don't perform for praise, attention or success.

30.Table: Primary and Secondary Reinforcers.

	Stimulus	Behavior	Consequence
Horse already knows	Whistle	Horse Comes	Primary reinforcer=carrots Paired with secondary reinforcer pat-pat
Horse will learn that the Pat-pat signals or cues that food is presented. This means the horse must learn what the pat-pat means.	Whistle	Horse Comes	Secondary reinforcer established The carrot with Pat-pat and sometimes the "stand in for the carrot" the pat-pat alone.

The important aspect is timing the pat-pat with the carrot. The horse thinks pat-pat=carrot. Here is where the "slap-pat-good horse" can make sense. Pat your horse (the "good horse" stuff is for your secondary reinforcer) and give the carrot. Now the "pat-slap-good horse" routine becomes a true reward in the eyes of the important one-your horse. The soothing voice combination also works as a secondary reinforcer. Another way to make this work is to use the "pat-pat" and "good horse" routine every time you feed your horse. Walk into the stall initiate the "pat-pat-soothing talk" and immediately dump the food. This is an example of a ideal way to pair the primary and secondary reinforcers. Remember food is at the heart of survival for animals and this is a perfect way to become part of that behavior.

14. Remember Pat-pat

Remember the pat and praise don't mean a thing–unless paired with something important to the horse

Schedules of Reinforcement

It would be nice if we were rewarded every single time we did something.

Most reinforcers happen some of the time, and unless someone like the trainer is aware of this important factor it may happen by chance. Part of this success of training with this method is that less will happen by chance. In laboratory experiments scientists discovered that schedules of reinforcement have a great effect on learning. As stated in part I, the effect of continuous reinforcement is helpful for the horse to learn the task. Also it was explained that the continuous reinforcement was useful in teaching the variations of the original task as the horse moved to a more complicated performance. Review Chapter 3 and the table:

"Horse putting on halter-Chain of behavior rewarded". Scientists discovered that behavior learned became more permanent if an Intermittent or partial reinforcement occurred. This means that the behavior is reinforced only some of the time. Remember the cartoon of the payoff of the one arm bandit? This is why gambling becomes so addictive because the behavior is reinforced only some of the time. Scientists also found that behavior that is intermittently reinforced is also very resistant to **extinction.**

I observed a student who rode a horse in a training clinic and by the time the lesson finished the horse was anticipating each time the student showed tiredness. As soon as the rider relaxed through the muscles of the seat and legs the horse was making transitions to the walk. The horse learned in that short period of time to recognize the cues. Horses are very consistent, if you do tasks 100% consistently they will never think of doing it another way, like other more intelligent animals but harder to train in this respect. Certainly this is one of the reasons that trainers must be very careful and patient with horse training. Horses often are easier to train in this respect because they are consistent in what they have learned and don't try inventive responses. The reader probably wouldn't be reading this book about training horses if you weren't patient-you would most likely have a motorcycle instead.

Part Three:

Horse Makeovers

Introduction: Horse Behavior Makeovers

> *So I would like to remind every rider to look to himself for the fault whenever he has difficulties with his horse.*
>
> —Podhajsky

Part I reviewed the basic principles that are needed to implement behavior modification for training horses. As discussed, behavior modification is a systematic procedure that is followed precisely using the principles outlined. As with all horse training, lessons need to be accurately completed to obtain results. Part I should be reviewed if the reader is unsure of any principles. Often retraining takes more time and effort than completing the correct work from the beginning. Behavior modification can be effectively used to correct problem training. The next pages give case studies of some problems that might be solved using systematic training as outlined. Several of the studies refer to dressage. Dressage (from the French "to train") provides basic sequential training objectives for the horse that lend themselves to horse training for any horse discipline.

In the following section a short horse profile will be described so the reader can understand some basic background for each horse. Each profile will list the following important elements for the solution of the problem including goals, objectives, and the behavior management tools that were explained in Part I:

- **Horse Profile**

  Provides some background in a personal narrative form to help the reader understand some of the characteristics and behavior of the horse described.

- **Description of behavior**

  Short statement about the behavior that is the concern or problem.

- **Goal**

  The overall statement of what we want the horse to do.

- **Objectives**

  Individual statements of specific observable behavior that leads the training procedure through a series of progressively harder objectives. to complete the goal.

- **Behavior Modification Tools**

  Choice of tools of behavior change or training, the individual reinforcers or aversive control that changes the behavior.

- **Summary**

  The closing statements and additional helpful information.

Horse Profile 1: The "Buffalo"

Horse Profile: The "Buffalo", as he was nicknamed in Germany, is a very large athletically strong, but pleasant and friendly-with-people horse. He is so even tempered that most unusual situations that provoke other horses don't bother him in the least. His training in dressage has been very successful, exemplified by a keen memory for lessons and eagerness to respond. Because of his powerful frame and not being overly sensitive, he often doesn't notice touch cues.

He is an example of the type of horse that tempts a trainer to use stronger and stronger aids to obtain a response. He is also an example of how doing an incorrect procedure with a clever horse may start the beginning of a poor habit. In addition the "Buffalo" demonstrates how aversive control or punishment will produce the opposite of the result desired.

Description of Behavior: The "Buffalo" has a natural ground covering stride that a handler encouraged by running him to the pasture. Buffalo began to become difficult going to and from the pasture wanting to go fast. The handler tried using stronger, aversive means to control him from going fast that were ineffective and made him act stronger against the aversive control.

Goal: To walk to a distant pasture under control of the handler.

Objectives: Each step leads to the next as it is considered learned.

- Walk the amount of steps that can be done correctly and stop with verbal cue
- Walk of few steps slowly and stop with a verbal cue
- Increase the amount of steps before stopping with verbal cue
- Increase the distance to halfway before stopping with verbal cue
- Walk the total distance to the pasture, walking as slow as the handler wants, stop with a verbal cue

Tool: Positive reinforcement

31. Table: Positive Reinforcement

Behavior	Stimulus Cue (remember this can be anything, sound, hand signal, etc. - the horse learns this signals reward	Consequence Reward or Positive reinforcer
Horse stops on verbal cue	Any sound etc.	Small tidbit

Summary: The reason that this method often fails is the improper timing of the reinforcer (Part I, cartoon of "Shakedown"). Remember the tidbit **isn't** taken by the horse, but given on the completion of the correct behavior paired with the cue. The trainer waits, making no movement, until the horse makes the correct response.

Horse Profile: The same horse from above.

Description of Behavior: Demonstrated lack of correct training for the aids of the reins during riding lessons. Was obedient to other aids.

Goal: Teach lightness in contact during the riding sessions.

Objectives:

(a) Lighten and yield contact as soon as the aid or cue for the reins is given (also called half halt).

(b) Lighten and yield contact for a few steps as soon as the aid or cue is given.

(c) Lighten and yield contact as soon as the aid or cue is given after keeping the 'lighten and yield' contact for one complete circle as soon as the aid or cue is given.

(d) Lighten and yield contact for longer periods of work as soon as the aid is given.

Tool: Negative Reinforcer

32. Table: Negative reinforcer

Stimulus signal or cue	Behavior	Consequence
Reins in contact with the horse's mouth	The horse yields and lightens contact	Reins release contact to the horse's mouth

Summary: Often this example fails because the rider doesn't release the pressure of the reins immediately after the horse yields. Sometimes the rider lacks basic riding skills allowing the hands to be steady and used independently of the seat. Balancing the rider's position using the reins often causes the horse to raise the head to protect against the harsh use of hands, because the negative reinforcer doesn't stop immediately upon the correct response by the horse.

15. Twinkle, twinkle...

Horse Profile: Buddy Games
Twinkle, twinkle little star....I wish my rider would let up on the reins

Horse Profile: When the "Buffalo" arrived from Germany he had his pasture friend with him. At two years going on three they both were still playing pasture buddy games with each other and occasionally their human companions. This game included moving his head around when humans were around and mock nipping and playing. Because his head was large it could be dangerous to have him moving it around when handlers were near. Interesting enough an expert local yahoo type visiting told me he would know how to handle this and give them both a good smack. The constant use of aversive control or punishment often encourages the animal or person to use the same aggression back on the aggressor. Aggression invites counter attack. Occasionally we hear about the tragedy of a horse whacking back. This doesn't mean that we let animal companions do whatever they want and become a nuisance or danger to others. There are instances where aversive control may be effectively used but it must be **carefully thought out, very sparingly** used., and **perfectly time.**. Needless to say we did not whack the "Buffalo" or his companion despite our expert local yahoo type's advice. Unfortunately, this type of behavior often seems to work and so these types of trainers are reinforced by their behavior. Reinforcers work for trainers as well.

33. Table: Reinforcement for Trainer

Stimulus	Behavior	Consequences
Horse misbehaving	Horse stops misbehaving when whacked by expert local yahoo type	Expert local yahoo type is reinforced and this behavior of whacking horses will increase. Other effective methods will not be tried or considered.

Aversive control doesn't have to be physical punishment to be effective. This was demonstrated in a hands-on way by a very intuitive trainer. During an extended time, I worked with him training several stallions. The stallions there were brought in from pastures to be trained and had many of the traits of playtime like the "Buffalo" and his friend. The voice was never raised except for a significant reason and this is how such young horse behavior was handled. When the young misbehaver made an aggressive action the trainer would yell in a loud voice the equivalent of stop. Nothing more aversive than a very loud voice timed with the action. We never had problems with the stallions started on his farm, only the ones that came in from other training. The effectiveness of the loud voice will be lost if used for every small infraction. Just like constantly yelling at kids, "Don't do that" and pretty soon they ignore you. The other reason for the effectiveness of this procedure is that the majority of behavior is handled in a positive way. A horse can't perform two opposite behaviors at the same time. As correct behavior increases inappropriate behavior decreases.

Description of Behavior: Demonstrated inappropriate horse-play actions toward human handlers.

Goal: Horse demonstrates human socially acceptable behavior.

Objective: Correct moment an unacceptable action was made toward the trainer-increase socially acceptable behavior

Behavioral Tools: Aversive Control; then positive reinforcers that increase the behaviors that the trainer wants. Incompatible behavior: if the correct behavior is reinforced, the undesirable behavior is deleted, so as the young horse becomes better trained the other incompatible behavior is dropped. Youngsters need to learn limits, and not becomes dangerous to others.

34. Table: punishing consequence

Undesired **Behavior**	Consequence Aversive Control
Nipping horseplay actions	Loud yell stop immediately paired with the undesired behavior

These are young horses that haven't learned to be vicious to human caretakers and are **very** different from an older horse that has learned to be dangerous to those around. Vicious human attacking behavior is a very different situation and needs professional advice.

Not only is the changing of the horse's behavior interesting in the previous case study but those of the trainers' as well. If we compare the reasons of the expert local yahoo type and real expert, we find that not only are appropriate behaviors of the trainers reinforced but inappropriate behavior. What increased the trainer's behavior? The horse by stopping the behavior increased the behavior of the trainers.

Behavioral Tools: Positive reinforcer-because the behavior that follows is increased–not positive for the horse but the trainer, because the trainer behavior is increased.

35. Table: Trainers Use Old Habits

Stimulus	Behavior	Consequences
Horse misbehaving	Horse stops misbehaving when whacked by expert yahoo type. (What often happens is the horse learns evasive behavior to avoid the whack).	Expert yahoo type is reinforced and this behavior of whacking horses will increase. Despite not knowing about other methods, the yahoo type will not consider that another tool might work more effectively
Horse misbehaving	Horse stops misbehaving when hearing a loud yell from real expert.	Real expert, is reinforced and continues to use this method to be effective with horses

16. Yardstick of behavior

Reasonable training

abusive	permissive

Horse Profile 2. "Diablo"

Horse Profile: Diablo means "devil" in Spanish. He was an attractive Spanish horse acquired by the Rodeo Club from the local horse market. He became their rodeo bronco for a while and when he no longer suited their purpose he was going to be put to sleep by the club because no one would purchase him. A young woman who took pity on him made the purchase, but was rightly afraid to ride him. He was going to be a pet temporarily until another solution could be found. Diablo was very gentle on the ground and very safe in this environment. His dual behavior was displayed when a human was on his back. In an open area, he would run for the nearest tree or fence and try to throw the rider. This was not going to be a short-term training session. No whispering in his ear and magically changing him. This was potentially dangerous behavior and no aversive control or punishment would reclaim his lost confidence. Again, as long as the trainer was on the ground he was the model horse being led and handled.

Description of Behavior: Dangerous behavior for the rider in the saddle because of lack of inappropriate beginning training (understatement for sure), and the extreme abusive handling, but totally pleasant and safe handling him on the ground.

Goal: Retrain Diablo to become a reliable pleasure horse through work on the ground using the longe line.

Objectives: Great care to assure each level was over learned before going to the next,

(a) Walk on the longe line moving away from the whip, stop on voice cue using a handler leading him to make sure the beginning behavior was perfectly learned with no mistakes.

(b) Walk on the longe with a handler leading him in a circle both directions moving away and forward from the whip and stopping on restraining of the longe line and voice commands. Practiced several days before moving to the next step

(c) Walk on the longe without a handler leading him in a circle both directions moving away and forward from the whip and stopping on restraint of the longe line and voice commands. Practiced several days before moving to the next step

(d) Walk on the longe without a handler leading him in a circle both directions moving away and forward from the whip and stopping on restraint of the longe line and voice commands. Using forward command of the whip to urge transition into the trot. Restraining cue paired with voice for a downward transition to the walk and then stop. Practiced several days before moving to the next step

(e) Wait until Diablo understood that the whip meant impulsion to go forward for the walk and trot and restraining transitions were made with the longe line and voice stop. (We waited until this work was thoroughly established before beginning the canter work so as not to evoke the possibility of old behavior that included excited running around behavior of bronco days).

(f) Canter resulted from understanding the move-forward aid and retraining aids thoroughly. Around the 3-month mark he was urged to go forward and stepped into the canter.

(g) Practiced all gaits walk, trot, and canter transitions thoroughly on the longe line preparing and reinforcing the aides of the whip and longe line that will eventually be transferred to the rider's reins and legs in the future.

Behavioral Tools: Both positive and negative reinforcers

36. Table: Positive and Negative Reinforcers

Stimulus or Cue	**Behavior**	Positive or Negative Reinforcer	Increases behavior
Whip raised	Move forward	Negative Reinforcer	Stop the use of the whip
Restraining longe	slow down	Negative Reinforcer	Stop the use of the longe line
This is behavior done to end session			
Voice cue to stop	Stop	Positive Reinforcer	Food reward

Summary: These tools were used to train the objectives each day for about 8 minutes on each side or ended when the trainer felt a behavior was well established. This small sequence was done for about 3 months to establish a new basis, trainer confidence, and a new pleasant routine. With retraining an especially difficult horse, there is no short cut. There is also no mystery, just the reinforcement of new behavior. This behavior becomes the new pattern and incompatible with the old behavior. Remember in the introduction discussing incompatible behaviors? A horse cannot be jumping around, biting and kicking, and going around in a calm manner at the same time. If the trainer rushes the work and the horse reverts to old habits the trainer will return to the original behavior and the old behavior will be strengthened by an effect called spontaneous recovery (means that the horse reverts to old habits and the behavior is reinforced; stronger than previously). Our friend Diablo found escape in his old habits from an aversive and punishing environment. These old behaviors were highly reinforced and it takes time to reinforce new behaviors.

The reason for using the longe line is the safety factor in retraining a horse that may be unpredictable and potentially dangerous for the rider. The trainer may observe correct behavior from the ground. The following goal and objectives are the main focus of work on the longe.

Goal: Produce a high quality riding horse for all disciplines

Objectives:

> Move forward from the whip.
> Restraining, downward transitions using the longe line.
> Obedience to voice commands.
> Practice upward transitions to trot and canter departures.
> Assist physical balance and athletic training in preparation for riding.

For a more in depth explanation of the details of beginning horses using longeing in this manner, the definitive work of the late Vienna school Director Podhajsky (1967, p. 14) explains the details and fine points of longe work. Walking behind a young untrained, horse, an unreliable horse in retraining or a high powered energetic mover isn't suitable for reinforcing the correct habits and is dangerous because of the position behind the horse. This work is safely accomplished using the basic longe work as described by Podhajsky.

Diablo became a fine riding horse with an especially easy to ride canter. Because of his nice behavior, Diablo was able to attract very nice owners. Actually, this was true of several other horses with problems of a lesser degree that used this positive approach to training. This method of longeing is different than other methods because it duplicates the aids of the rider while providing the safety of working from the ground and at a safe distance. Instead of merely exercising the horse it progressively teaches obedience to the rider's aids. The trainer doesn't chase the horse but the horse goes forward because he has learned the cue of the raised whip. It also allows the horse to learn transitions without the weight of the rider. This is a positive situation for the horse; nothing is done out of mysterious actions, but cues that are taught by the trainer and learned by the horse.

17. Two Faced Horse

Incompatible behaviors can't be performed at the same time

Horse Profile 3: "Xerxio"

Horse Profile: Xerxio is a sensitive highly talented Lusitano that was destined to be a bull fighting horse in Portugal when fate intervened and he became mine. He easily learned and performs passage, piaffer, levade, flying change, extended trot-Spanish trot, and Spanish walk. From the time he was almost three he was wonderful to work with even with his overly sensitive nature. This profile is an example of how aversive control can have disastrous results. This event happened at the hands of a small town Spanish farrier, who ran a nail into the sensitive area of the hoof and continued with aversive control by roughly restraining him. This traumatized the horse beyond any way to get him shod including tranquilizing. At this point, the mere sound of the tools became the cue. He still performed beautifully and I could handle his hoofs but as soon as a hammer tapped his hoof he became completely unmanageable. There also was an additional cue of the strong restraining method that the blacksmith used holding the hoof. As long as the hoof was held lightly in the hand he was perfectly calm. It took only minutes to create this problem and almost a year of continued work to restore total confidence.

Description of Behavior: Could not use farrier tools to hammer on shoes

Goal: to restore confidence so that the horse could be shod

Objectives:

(a) Shoes removed and only hoof pick and rasp work used.

(b) Only hoof pick and rasp work used, hoof tapped lightly with a hoof pick

(c) Only hoof pick and rasp work used, tapped with a light hammer

(d) Only hoof pick and rasp work used, tapped with a light hammer light restraining hoof between the knees like most blacksmith used to apply shoes

37. Table: Tools-Positive Reinforcer

Stimulus	Behavior	Positive Reinforcer
Tapping the hoof	Horse staying calm	Primary reinforcer given Secondary reinforcers given on an intermittent schedule

Summary: Many times horse owners must rely on other sources such as farrier, vets, and boarding facilities. Often owners must be absent during what may seem like routine procedures. Horse handlers who routinely use aversive measures may put horses at risk as exemplified in this case. Once aversive controls go wrong, a compounding effect encourages horse handlers to attempt to use more force to solve the problem. It often seems like a quick fix as compared with the time spent to successfully reconstruct the desired behavior. This isn't to say that aversive control is never used, but that it is very carefully thought out with full understanding of the outcomes. The last objective was to find an understanding farrier to put on shoes. A German farrier had an assistant hold the hoof lightly so as not to restrain the leg. Since that time there have been no reoccurring problems.

18. The Visit

*You asked **both** to come at the **same** time?*

Key Points

- The purpose of this section was to provide some personal accounts using real happenings to demonstrate how behavioral modification techniques may be use to intervene and change behavior.

- Readers can see a model for delineating behavior so they may work up a behavioral approach to solving any problem. Behavior modification is a definite way of approaching observable horse behavior and a systematic way of thinking about creating the performance we want.

- All behavior increases or decreases depending on what follows the event. Understanding the tools of behavior modification that communicate your wishes is essential.

- Your horse training will never happen by chance and the latest clinic or training session will make sense for the reason it works or doesn't work.

- There are no perfect horses or trainers, but there are methods that will bring each one closer to that goal and do it in a happy positive environment using the tools of behavioral modification.

- Behavior modification is an equitable approach that is neither permissive nor abusive and treats both the trainer and horse with respect.

Last words:
Think before you act: How will this help increase or decease the behavior I want from my horse and what am I doing that encourages this to happen?

After word

There are two major outcomes from the use of the material contained in this book:

1. The creation and change of behavior
2. A positive relationship between horse and rider/trainer

Behavior modification is a very strong tool that if used correctly can create a positive learning environment. The information presented, provides the resources to change and teach desired behavior. The material describes the method to generate not only preferred behavior from your horse, but a contented attitude and preservation of a happy relationship.

Much of what is done to horses at best can be called unpleasant. Would you willingly stay in surroundings where the only contacts and handling were disagreeable?

We so often hear, "My horse doesn't like to work". Perhaps the answer is because the only pleasant thing associated with the training happens when the trainer leaves and the horse goes back to the stall or pasture.

The purpose of this material is to help trainers to:

1. Move away from mysterious methods of viewing horse behavior
2. Define horse behavior in specific goals and objectives
3. Use behavior modification techniques to positively reinforce and support desired horse behavior

A prospective publisher told me that this material is too academic for equestrians. I don't believe this is true. Most equestrians spend a great deal of time, effort, and money to become better informed. Often these resources are wasted because of the shallowness of the subject content. I offer the information of scientific research, and behavioral analysis condensed into an easier to understand application that is specific to horses. Simply stated:

1. Trainers need to identify a very simple observable achievable behavior
2. Using reinforcers, desired behavior is encouraged to repeat

The final outcome of using a positive approach to horse training is that the trainer begins to observe behavior, change their own behavior, and take responsibility for the behavior of their horse.

About the Author

Patti Dammier has the
best of both worlds as a
professional educator
and Grand Prix dressage
trainer and competitor.
Her degrees in education
include a masters and
continued doctorial
studies in educational
methods and research.
Concerned about the
lack of behavioral
literature describing the

training of horses Patti continues to collect data and write about
the use of behavior science for training horses. With over 25 years
as a professional educator, teaching behavior modification
programs to create optimal learning environments, she is an
expert not only teaching methods but horse training as well.
Behavior modification brings the dependability of a consistent
approach to develop a positive approach to learning and training
environments. Horses need to have the comfort of knowing what
is expected and the consistency of methodical training instead of
the latest fad. Living more than half of her life in Europe afforded
Patti the opportunity to study riding in the best schools in Spain,
Portugal, England, and Germany. Not only does she have riding
and training expertise but the knowledge to use behavior
modification to implement those skills.

Quality education consists of knowledge and not a series of faddish shortcuts. Knowledge of the basic principles of behavior modification provides the groundwork to teach horses the behavior we want and make our relationships with horses positive.

If you would like to know more about behavior modification for horses check the internet site at:http://www.gotcarrots.com

Patti with Xerxio, a Portuguese Lusitano

Notes

Dog training makes use of the secondary reinforcers as described by Ferster, Culberstson, and Boren "In Behavior Principles" (p.36) by using a cricket to stand for rewards. To summarize: The dog has food placed in a bowl and immediately hears the sound of the cricket. After several repetitions the sound of the cricket has become a secondary reinforcer and stands in for food. Every time the dog hears the cricket he receives a secondary reinforcer. The trainer then proceeds teach a routine by sending him to do a task-like go to a spot in the room. Each time the dog makes a move toward the desired spot the cricket is sounded, and the behavior is reinforced. If the behavior increases the secondary reinforcer is successful. The book also explains that there is a socialization aspect of secondary reinforcers with dogs that isn't apparent with cats. I would add that it is different for horses too.

For the most part it is unnecessary to use only one cue or secondary reinforcer for horses because they aren't "sent" to a spot (Review Rider Aids and Devices). Horses are taught a variety of routines and are more successfully reinforced by using the various objects connected with each task as the cue or secondary reinforcer.

Glossary

Aversive control or punishment An unpleasant consequence following a behavior that results in termination of the behavior.

Behavior A single event of observable or measurable behavior.

Behavior Modification The application of the principles of conditioning to changing behavior.

Behavior science The systematic study of the behavior of organisms. Horses like all animals, including us, tend to repeat pleasurable happenings and avoid those that are unpleasant.

Behaviorism An approach to psychology that studies observable behavior and the role of the environment as a determinant of behavior.

Behavior modification A system for the appraisal and change of behavior.

Consequence Out comes or results of actions and behavior.

Contingencies The conditions under which specific reinforcer are applied to behavior.

Classical conditioning The systematic and sometimes by chance application of contingencies to behavior that are reflexes. For horses it is important that the flight reflex isn't paired with a chance cue.

Cue An event that signals that a particular behavior will be reinforced. It's useful to create cues that may be used both on the ground and in the saddle.

Environment The surroundings that support learning. When beginning a task the environment is created so that the desired behavior is promoted.

Goals A broadly described statement or aim about a behavioral activity. Often these goals are so broadly stated that I'd difficult to make them obtainable. An example for a beginning rider would be:" I will ride my horse in a local schooling show".

Natural reflexes or instincts Responses such as salivation, breathing, suckling, and flight. They are considered behaviors necessary for survival.

Negative reinforcers An aversive event that when stopped increases the response that terminate the aversive event. Rider aids are negative reinforcers that when immediately released, increased the behavior that stops the mildly unpleasant effect (when correctly performed).

Objectives The observable behavior single event or action that leads to the goal. A useful objective state includes a description of what the learner is expected to do, conditions and the level of competence (Mager p.52).

Operant conditioning The systematic arranging or operations that produce a behavior that is created through the application contingencies that allow new behavio4 to be formed.

Primary reinforcers For horses primary reinforcers are food because it doesn't depend on learning for it's reinforcing attributes

Reinforcers Those consequences that strengthen the response or increase the rate of responding.

Rewards of positive reinforcers A pleasurable consequence after a behavior that will increase the rate of responding.

Stimulus A signal or some kind of cue present-could be visual, sound, or smell.

Schedules of reinforcement A decision made about how many or which response will be reinforced.

Secondary reinforcers. In contrast to primary reinforcers, secondary reinforcers depend on learning. They are cues or symbols that have been attached to primary reinforcers by training and previous experience. The pat-pat/good horse becomes a secondary reinforcer when the pat-pat was previous don while giving a primary reinforcer, example-a carrot.

Successive approximation Responses that are reinforced as they more closely approached the final desired behavior.

References

Bekoff, M. & Byers, J. A. (1998). *Animal play: Evolutionary and ecological perspectives.* London: Cambridge University Press.

De la Guérinière, F. R. (1994). *School of horsemanship.* London: J. A. Allen & Co.

De la Guérinière, F. R. (1733). *Ecole de cavalerie.* Paris: Collombat.

Gianoli, L.(1969).*Horses and horsemanship through the ages.* New York: Crown Publishers, Inc.

Kazdin, A. E. (1975). *Behavior modification in applied settings.* Homewood, II: The Dorsey Press.

Klimke, R. (1969). *Cavaletti.* Canaan, NY: J.A. Allen & Co.

Mager, R. F. (1997). *Preparing instructional objectives.* Alanta , GA: The Center for Effective Performance, Inc
Podhajsky, A (1965). *The complete training of horse and rider.* Garden City, NY: Doubleday & Company, Inc.

Podhajsky, A (1969). *My horses, my teachers.* Garden City, NY: Doubleday & Company, Inc.

Podhajsky, A (1974). *The riding teacher.* London: Harrap & Co.

Olivera, N. (1976). *Reflections on equestrian art.* London: J. A. Allen.

Skinner, B. F. (1953). *Science and Human Behavior.* New York: The Free Press.

Skinner, B.F (!974). *About behaviorism.* New York: Alfred A. Knopf.

Weiten, W.(1989).*Psychology themes and variations.* Pacific Grove, CA: Brooks/Cole Publishing Company.

Xenophon, *On horsemanship.* Written in fourth century B.C.

Index